EXECUTIVE COACHING

EXECUTIVE COACHING

Building and Managing Your
Professional Practice

LEWIS R. STERN

WILEY

John Wiley & Sons, Inc.

Library of Congress Cataloging-in-Publication Data:

Stern, Lewis R.
    Executive coaching: building and managing your professional practice/by
Lewis R. Stern.
    p. cm.
Includes index.
ISBN 978-0-470-17746-4 (cloth)
    1. Executive coaching. I. Title.
    HD30.4.S74 2008
    658.4'07124 — dc22

                                                                    2008002753

Printed in the United States of America.

10 9 8 7 6 5 4 3 2 1

Contents

Contents

Contents

Preface

This book is the product of 30 exciting years of professional learning. In those 30 years, I have been privileged to work with thousands of leaders and experts in coaching and consulting around the world. The book is also informed by my recent work in several capacities including: cofounder and chairman of the executive coaching forum; co-founder and board member of the Graduate School Alliance for Executive Coaching; founder, director, and faculty member of the Graduate Certificate Program in Executive Coaching at the Massachusetts School of Professional Psychology; and chairman of the Global Convention on Coaching's Working Group on Guidelines for Coach Training. The book is a practical, how-to guide for people from diverse backgrounds who are interested in exploring, building, expanding, or better managing their professional practice in executive coaching. I believe this information will be valuable to management consultants, organization development specialists, human resources professionals, and coaches with other specialties. *External* consultants working from outside the client's organization, either independently or as part of a consulting firm or group, will find this book a useful guide. *Internal* consultants, or employees in the organization where their coaching clients work, will discover practical approaches and resources to build and manage their coaching practices from within their organizations.

My motivation for writing this book came from several sources. It has been frustrating to see many people call themselves executive coaches when they do not have the knowledge or expertise to serve their clients well. They have lowered the standards of quality as perceived by coaching clients and the public. I have had the privilege of working with professional executive coaches from varied backgrounds; many of them masters of the art as well as experts in the evidence-based nature of coaching leaders and would-be leaders around the world. I learn from them every day as they establish the highest of standards on which the evolving discipline of executive coaching is built.

There are many talented people in executive coaching who believe in setting rigid entry standards into the field. They maintain that the only people who can do executive coaching are professionals just like them. I do not believe that every executive coach needs to have a master's or doctorate degree in a specific field, 20 years of experience working in different industries, or a senior executive background. I do believe, however, that a base of knowledge, ability, skills, and attributes is required for anyone to do professional executive coaching as it is defined in this book. I also believe that not every executive coach has to be able to handle every possible coaching situation. Smart people with the right attributes and abilities can learn to be good coaches. This book helps you to assess whether you have these attributes and abilities and what you need to learn or compensate for to be a successful executive coach.

My final motivation for writing this book came from the graduate students and coaches I teach and supervise. Each student arrives with a passion for the field coupled with a lack of confidence about coaching. In their two years of extensive study, these students not only learn theory, principles, and practices—they also gain awareness about themselves and discover how to use their strengths and focus their practice accordingly. But each student also craves practical guidance for building and managing a coaching practice. That is the purpose of this book.

As I wrote this book, I often found myself trying to decide if I should take a stance on a topic I feel strongly about even though others in the field disagree with me. I decided to express my beliefs and opinions without apologizing or feeling obligated to represent other views. Read this book as one professional's perspective and recommended approaches to executive coaching. I also encourage you to consider differing perspectives and recommendations from other experts in the field.

This book is about what I and others have found to work best when building and managing a professional executive coaching practice. Chapter 1 starts by helping you decide if executive coaching is the right match for you. It offers some shared definitions of the field before getting into the nitty-gritty of what an executive coach actually does. I compare executive coaching to other forms of coaching and to counseling and psychotherapy, contrasting the competencies all coaches need with the specific competencies of executive coaches. Since the core of the definition of executive coaching I use is the double focus on leadership development and accomplishing organizational results, I review common goals for each of these objectives. Chapter 1 also provides checklists of what to do before, during, and after coaching; how to match a leader with the right coach; the role of the human resources professional in executive coaching; what actually takes place in executive coaching sessions; an overview of how to market your coaching services; and some suggestions on how to use this book to start or expand your professional practice as an executive coach.

Chapter 2 provides a detailed self-assessment and 360-degree survey to help you identify your strengths and opportunities for development as an executive coach. It includes a template for your professional development plan.

Chapter 3 gives you a step-by-step guide to creating your value proposition as an executive coach and developing and marketing your practice. This plan is based on not only your business goals, but also your personal and career goals. The marketing plan helps you define your target market and build a plan to penetrate it through networking and a consultative selling approach. Guidelines are provided for an array of marketing approaches including market research, marketing materials, e-mail, the Web, targeted mailings, presentations, publishing, advertising, and partnerships and referral sources.

Chapter 4 is a guide to assembling and managing the building blocks of your practice: a coaching network, toolbox, office infrastructure, coaching project management system, professional and peer supervision, research and publication, and community service. The guide is detailed with specific options, suggestions, and examples of coaching tools, office space, data and file management, technology, project scoping, conducting chemistry checks with potential clients, contracting, assessments, and developing and managing a coaching project plan.

Chapter 5 helps you transition from other professional disciplines or coaching specialties: mental health, business management, organization development and management consulting, personal/life coaching, and internal human resources roles. Key strengths from each field are identified as well as potential barriers, and strategies to make the transition from each specialty into executive coaching are discussed.

Chapter 6 puts it all together and helps you develop a detailed plan for your professional executive coaching practice.

The Appendix is an extensive listing of resources available to executive coaches. It includes articles and books, journals, organizations, web sites, assessments, and tools. These resources are based on my personal experience and the recommendations from over 40 leaders in the field throughout the United States and the world.

As I began to write this book, I intended for it to focus solely on the building and managing of your coaching practice. But much of what I and others have found to be critical to the success of a professional executive coach is how to conduct the actual coaching and support our coaching clients. As a result, this book has ended up being as much about the coaching itself as it is about building and managing a coaching practice.

If you are looking for an academic treatise on research and standards, I encourage you to look elsewhere. This book is for the practical professional with a passion for helping leaders do great things through executive coaching. I wish you the same satisfaction that I continue to experience in my work as a professional executive coach.

Acknowledgments

Executive coaching did not really exist as a defined field when I began my work. I started as a consulting psychologist, counseling, coaching, training, and consulting in education and mental health. Three of my mentors, Murray Sholkin, Steve Sholkin, and Harry Levinson, encouraged me to apply my knowledge to the business world. I owe them all a debt of gratitude for expanding my horizons on where and how to practice.

My work in business started as training and slowly expanded into coaching and consulting. I learned so much about management, leadership, and organization development through my 9 years of work with colleagues at ODI, consulting to leaders in many industries on a global basis. My colleagues at Manchester Consulting made important contributions to the development of executive coaching systems and processes, and I owe them a great deal for sharing their experience and expertise. In the two consulting firms I have run, Focus Consulting and Stern Consulting, I have had the opportunity to work with wonderful clients and tenured professionals in all types of coaching and consulting. My thanks go to all of them for their generosity in sharing their knowledge, expertise, and support.

My professional network has inspired much of this book. I thank my colleagues and friends from the Executive Coaching Forum, the New England Society for Applied Psychology, the Massachusetts School of Professional Psychology, the Graduate School Alliance for Executive Coaching, and the Global Convention on Coaching. Special thanks go to my cowriters of the Executive Coaching Forum's *Executive Coaching Handbook* and *Core Competencies of the Executive Coach,* the foundation on which so much of this book rests. Beyond these more formal groups, there are so many other people from whom I continually learn and receive support. Thank you all for easing the loneliness of the executive coach with your community of shared learning. I would also thank all of my students and supervisees for teaching me through their own wisdom and learning.

As I worked on compiling the Appendix for this book, I found it especially interesting that professionals from different backgrounds and geographic locations recommended very different resources. Executive coaching is truly a diverse discipline.

I have learned about the professional practice of executive coaching from so many sources. Each of them has informed me in my thinking and the resources I use. I cannot acknowledge all of those people here; instead I list the individuals who responded to my request to recommend resources for this book. Thanks to them all for their serious consideration and time in providing their recommendations:

Chris Anderson, United States
John Bennet, United States
Jennifer Garvey Berger, New Zealand
Bob Bonnevie, United States
Dianne Brennan, United States
Gabriele Buzatu, Australia
Alain Cardon, France
Naiomi Deutscher, United States
Susan Ennis, United States
Gabriele Ganswindt, United States
Susan Glynn, United States
Robert Goodman, United States
Diana Hammer, United States
William Hodgetts, United States

Acknowledgments

James Hunt, United States
Judy Ingalls, United States
Wendy Johnson, United States
Carol Kauffman, United States
Tomas Kottner, Argentina
Martie Lancellas, South Africa
Madeleine Mcbrearty, Canada
Kathleen Naylor, United States
Aletta Odendaal, South Africa
Ruth Orenstein, United States
Linda Page, United States
Carol Pelissey, United States
David Peterson, United States
Susie Rheault, United States
David Rock, Australia
Ann Rogers, United States
Bill Roiter, United States
Anne Scoular, United Kingdom
Larry Starr, United States
Reinhard Stelter, Denmark
Monica Sullivan, United States
JB Symons, United States
Michele Vitti, United States
Mary Watts, United Kingdom
Gil Williams, United States
Ellen Wingard, United States
Robert Witherspoon, United States

Marquita Flemming, Senior Editor at John Wiley & Sons, Inc., deserves my gratitude for her great support, especially in the final stages of preparing the manuscript for publication. And I thank Larissa Hordynsky, independent editor, for working closely with me to transform my often less-than-clear or consistent words into more articulate text.

As part of my "day job," I have written many handbooks, training manuals, articles, and tools for my clients, students, and other coaches and consultants. When I began to develop this book, however, it quickly became evident that I would have to take time away from family and friends. I thank them all for their unfailing encouragement. My daughters have been the greatest of supports, with Abbie, the younger, serving as my editor and formatter as I began to pull the book together. And of course my dog Samantha was always beside me as I wrote, inspiring me and exerting her calming influence whenever papers flew or the computer malfunctioned yet again.

The person who has shown the greatest patience and support for my work, even when it took time away from the rest of our life, is my wife Jean. She is my coach and mentor. I thank her for being there for me every step of the way, in this process and in our life.

CHAPTER ONE

Is Executive Coaching Right for You?

Many people are attracted to the field of executive coaching. After all, as a coach you are regarded as an expert with the ability to help others succeed and be happy at their game. Doing anything called "executive" sounds professional, smart, and prestigious. As an executive coach with several decades of experience and director of a graduate program in Executive Coaching, I get calls just about every week from a wide variety of people wanting to enter the field.

Exciting and satisfying as it is, this field is not for everybody. To qualify as an executive coach, you need certain attributes as well as a great deal of education, preparation, experience, continuous learning, and support. I have written this book to help—whether you are considering getting into the field; preparing to practice; or already practicing and looking for guidance, strategies, tools, and resources to build and manage your consultancy. This is not an academic study of the history of executive coaching nor does it contain a detailed discussion of the theory of executive coaching. Rather, this is a practical guide based on my experience as one professional, coupled with the advice many of my colleagues have shared with me.

What Is Executive Coaching?

Let's begin by examining what makes executive coaching different from other forms of coaching, counseling, and consulting. In the work I have been privileged to do as a member of a number of groups of experts in the field of executive coaching, there have been several key attributes that define and separate executive coaching from other kinds of consulting. Most executive coaching is done with leaders or would-be leaders of organizations. (A leader is loosely defined as anyone working in an organization who can have significant influence on the mission, direction, strategy, or long-term success of that organization.) Historically, although the term *executive coaching* has most commonly referred to this type of work, it is not in any way restricted to coaching people considered to be "executives."

The organizations that provide executive coaching range from big businesses to small family-owned enterprises, from government agencies to hospitals, nonprofits to universities, and public and private schools to venture capital firms, law firms, and advertising agencies. Certain industries, such as high technology and financial services, began using executive coaching as early as the 1980s and 1990s. Most industry sectors have jumped on the bandwagon by now, with a good number of organizations providing coaching. The industries that got an earlier start appear to be doing more proactive, developmental coaching for people with high potential, or those entering critical roles, or expanding their leadership responsibilities.

Five to 10 years ago, executive coaching was primarily remedial in nature: "fixing" people, solving performance problems, or putting out fires set by poor leadership. Today, that pattern has reversed itself, with most organizations focusing their executive coaching on developing leadership capabilities and achieving strategic organizational results in a proactive fashion. Some industries and organizations that have only recently embraced executive coaching are just beginning to focus on proactive development and results versus remediation. But there is no question that just about all industries and types of organizations are providing executive coaching. Given these varied client groups and coaching mandates, the work of the executive coach often overlaps with the larger scopes of leadership development, organization development, and management consulting.

A basic definition of executive coaching is derived from the work of the Graduate School Alliance for Executive Coaching (2007, p. 1) and the Executive Coaching Forum (2004, p. 19):

> Executive coaching is a development process that builds a leader's or would-be leader's capabilities to achieve professional and organizational goals. This coaching is conducted through one-on-one and group interactions, driven by evidence/data from multiple perspectives, and is based on mutual trust and respect. The coach, individuals being coached, and their organizations work in partnership to help achieve the agreed upon goals of the coaching.

This approach to developing leaders and facilitating organizational results can be provided by line managers, human resources professionals, management consultants, training and development professionals, and just about anyone in the position to help others become better leaders and achieve results. The executive coach for whom this book is written is not just someone who coaches leaders and tries to accomplish these goals. Rather, it takes a highly educated and trained professional who is well prepared to tackle any client's needs in these areas. Successful practitioners must have access to a wide variety of resources, plus a system, process, and support to provide executive coaching according to professional standards as described in this book.

Job of the Professional Executive Coach

Executive coaching is one of the many approaches in the repertoire management and leadership consultants employ. Consultants assess organizational situations and help the leaders and members involved improve their effectiveness and results. Some consultants do a lot of one-on-one and group development, advising leaders and would-be leaders in client organizations. When they are applying those approaches, consultants are serving as executive coaches. They consider themselves, or are considered by others, to be professional executive coaches for several reasons.

Professional executive coaching has four defining factors:

1. Executive coaches often focus a great deal of their consulting practice on one-on-one and group coaching.
2. They often employ a more structured process in their coaching work, such as following a set protocol of precoaching activities, assessment, and goal setting.
3. Their clients may seek them out specifically for executive coaching, asking them to follow the organization's guidelines or other standards for coaching.
4. They may contract for coaching work differently than for other consulting projects when it comes to confidentiality, data gathering, communication, project management, payment, and other terms and logistics of their work.

Many coaches who work with people on personal, career, financial, or other issues aspire to do executive coaching. Their motivations are as diverse as the coaches themselves. Some want to make more money. Others are fascinated by the challenges of business or organizational leadership. And still others are seeking prestige or the stimulation of working with especially smart and interesting people. But just imagine that you are a financial coach with a background in accounting or investment strategies. Your ability to help your clients depends not only on your basic coaching skills but, perhaps more importantly, on possessing the knowledge and expertise each unique client needs. When you work with a young couple just starting to invest for their children's education or their own retirement, or to ensure care for their aging parents, you must be knowledgeable and experienced in all of these areas. If your client's needs require you to have special knowledge in areas in which you lack expertise, such as international bonds or eldercare law, then you must be able to refer your client to a reliable resource network.

Similarly, as an executive coach you must have basic knowledge and experience of what most leaders and would-be leaders know and do. You need as much education, training, and experience in the specialty areas of executive coaching as the financial coach has in finance. Whether you are a personal coach, career coach, financial coach, or training and development specialist, you will not be effective as an executive coach without the requisite education, training, and expertise.

Executive Coaches Are Different

Professional executive coaches have much in common with many coaches (sports, academic, personal, career, spiritual, marital, financial, communication, parenting, and so many others). Most, regardless of their specialization:

- Work one-on-one and with small groups of people
- Help clients understand what they want to accomplish and what it will take to accomplish it
- Provide expertise and guidance to help clients improve themselves, change their behaviors, make decisions, plan to accomplish their goals, and carry through with those plans
- Reassure and help clients build and maintain self-confidence and a positive attitude in the face of difficult challenges, self-doubt, and emotional lows as well as high stress and new opportunities
- Provide focus, validate, do reality testing, and help clients think differently to break out of mental mindsets and be innovative

All coaches provide this help by bringing to the coaching relationship sound and basic coaching skills as well as a strong base of knowledge and expertise in their area of specialization. The best tennis coaches are not only good at these activities, but they also know a lot about the game of tennis and are experienced in helping tennis players improve their technique and develop strategies against opponents with a variety of strengths and weaknesses. Executive coaches must also have a great deal of expertise and experience in leadership, learning, organizations, people, business, and many other areas.

Executive coaches have two basic goals as they work with their clients:

1. Help build the leadership capabilities and effectiveness of the individuals coached, and
2. Help those individuals achieve organizational results.

Many other types of coaches work with leaders and would-be leaders in organizations. They do not, however, focus on these two goals. Presentation coaches, for example, improve leaders' presentation skills. Time management coaches show people how to organize their time and work. Career coaches help leaders step back and decide where to go professionally and how to get there. Life coaches help people who happen to be leaders think about their lives, plan to achieve their goals, and lead their lives with success and satisfaction. Although executive coaches often use these and other approaches, what makes their work different is their primary focus on leadership development and organizational results.

Executive Coaching versus Counseling and Psychotherapy

There is often overlap between counseling and psychotherapy on the one hand and executive coaching on the other. Counseling and psychotherapy focus primarily on helping people understand themselves, lead productive lives, and deal with personal challenges or mental health problems that stand in the way of happiness and positive relationships. The goal is to help people sort out how they think, feel, and behave—and how they would like to think, feel, and behave—before shaping satisfying and productive lives for themselves and those with whom they interact. The focus of the work is on the personal versus the professional, on what goes on inside the client's head and body, how to interact with family and friends, and how to concentrate on the positive and solve problems that interfere with life and happiness. People learn to recognize and manage their difficulties themselves, with their counselor or therapist helping them identify opportunities and capitalize on them.

Therapeutic Challenges of Counseling and Psychotherapy

Counselors and psychotherapists, who usually have clinical or counseling backgrounds in psychology, psychiatry, social work, or related fields, deal with such issues as helping people:

- Achieve calmness or dealing with anxiety
- Handle mood/depression
- Set personal goals or priorities
- Improve family or personal relationships
- Deal with problems sleeping, eating, or thinking clearly
- Accept and resolving difficult experiences or traumas
- React emotionally to physical illness
- Manage stress
- Learn new ways to deal with personal differences, limitations, or challenges
- Resolve personal or interpersonal conflict
- Have realistic expectations from life
- Learn positive new habits, breaking old ones, or changing behaviors
- Learn more productive ways to live life and overcome personal barriers
- Make the most of their lives

Some of these personal challenges can act as barriers to or opportunities for accomplishing the goals of executive coaching. Leaders may find it difficult to be patient with people they manage due partly to anxiety or problems with personal relationships. Key leaders on project teams may overcommit and manage time inefficiently because of a learning disability or personal challenges that prevent multitasking. When personal differences and problems require more long-term and clinical interventions, you as executive coach should refer the coachee to a qualified mental-health professional. If such problems significantly interfere with the ability to achieve work or coaching goals, you may not be able to help unless the problems are resolved through personal coaching, counseling, or psychotherapy.

Too often executive coaches try to take on therapeutic challenges. And mental-health professionals who try to provide executive coaching often look for, diagnose, and treat personal problems from a clinical perspective. Short coaching excursions into personal issues may help move a coaching agenda forward, but bigger, more therapeutic issues should be dealt with outside the coaching relationship by a mental-health professional.

Keep in mind that as executive coach, your primary obligation is to the organization that hired you. Your obligation is not to help executives deal with personal problems or lead happier lives, but to develop them into successful leaders capable of achieving results for their organization. There are times when you, with the permission of your coachee, can collaborate with a counselor, personal coach, psychotherapist, psychologist, social worker, psychiatrist, or other qualified mental-health worker. These professionals will keep you, and each other, informed while supporting your client's personal and professional development. The wall of confidentiality they maintain will not interfere with the rights and safety of the individual nor your obligations to the organization where the coachee works. Separating personal development goals and who helps to achieve them will avoid conflicts of interest between your commitments to the individual and the organization.

Major Differences between Executive Coaching and Counseling or Psychotherapy

- Coaching is primarily focused on practical, action-oriented goals; counseling and psychotherapy are primarily focused on helping people understand themselves and change the way they manage their lives.

- Coaching is most often focused on building skills and plans and implementing them; counseling and psychotherapy focus on gaining greater self-awareness and exploring better ways to cope with personal difficulties, challenges, and opportunities.
- Coaching is usually short term, with a goal of improving or achieving a specific outcome. Although some forms of counseling and psychotherapy are short term, it usually takes many months or years to deal with significant emotional issues or ingrained personal tendencies.
- Coaching is about identifying goals, opportunities to learn, and solutions. Counseling and psychotherapy focus on identifying personal needs, opportunities, and problems. Therapists help their clients to meet needs, capitalize on opportunities, solve problems, and develop life strategies to cope with or compensate for problems that cannot be solved.

COACHING COMPETENCIES

Regardless of the coaching specialty, all coaches must be able to:

- Build trust
- Ask useful questions
- Actively listen
- Guide
- Problem solve
- Generate creative solutions
- Provide emotional and motivational support
- Demonstrate skills and best practices
- Give constructive feedback
- Show enthusiasm
- Inspire self-confidence and encouragement
- Organize
- Plan
- Follow through

- Establish coaching goals
- Monitor coaching results
- Develop coaching strategies and adjust them as the coaching progresses

Special Knowledge and Skills of Executive Coaches

Professional executive coaches need specialty knowledge and expertise in five sets of competencies: psychology, business acumen, organization development, executive coaching knowledge and skills, and consulting practice development and management. Chapter 2 of this book describes each of these areas and shows you how to assess yourself, obtain feedback, and evaluate others. Chapter 2 will also help you identify strengths to build on and to identify gaps in knowledge and skills to fill before you can succeed as an executive coach. Let's begin with a general description of each set of competencies.

PSYCHOLOGY   Executive coaching focuses on helping individuals be effective leaders and achieve results for their organizations. To help a leader, you must understand how adults think, feel, and behave; what drives them; how they learn and change; how they interact with and influence others; and what differentiates them individually, in relationship to other individuals, and as members of groups. In addition, knowledge about the science and professional practice of psychology provides a data-based, valid, and ethical orientation. Many sets of psychological skills transfer to executive coaching, helping you assess people and situations, provide feedback, teach, advise, and collaborate with others to build capabilities and solve problems.

BUSINESS ACUMEN   Executive coaching takes place within the context of a business organization. The business within which your client operates may take many forms; a for-profit corporation, non-profit, school, government agency, hospital or health-care practice, or small family owned business. Since executive coaching focuses

10

on helping the coachee lead within the business and achieve business results, you as coach must understand how businesses operate and leaders achieve results in a variety of business settings. Knowledge and skills are essential in business principles and practices, finance, customers, management and supervision of employees, business functions and roles, technologies, current trends in the local and global marketplace, and human resources management.

ORGANIZATIONAL DEVELOPMENT Executive coaching must take place within the context of the organization in which the client leads or will lead. Therefore it is essential for you, as a professional, to understand how organizational systems operate and develop; their structures, systems, cultures, subgroups, and leadership practices. Besides a solid grasp of the theory behind organization development, you must also possess the strategies and techniques to help your client assess, intervene, facilitate in, and develop the organization. Without these skills, you cannot help your coachee become a better leader, bring about change, and achieve results within the organization.

Defining and Setting Standards for Executive Coaching

Ten years ago hardly a book or professional article was available on executive coaching; practically no research had been done on the topic. There was no agreement on what executive coaching was and little, if any, education and training for coaches. The discipline is still in its formative stages, but it is moving toward global agreement on defining and setting standards for the education, training, and practice of executive coaching. Our knowledge grows every day as experts share their theories, approaches, stories, and results. There are now hundreds of books and articles on executive coaching, with more coming out each month. To serve your clients well, you must be educated on the foundation of your discipline and keep up with emerging knowledge about theories, principles, practices, data, tools, and skills.

Executive coaches need to understand the wide variety of multidisciplinary models and theories of coaching. You cannot help a client without forming your own theoretical model. Besides developing integrity and good judgment, learn to approach executive coaching from a systems perspective, with a focus on business and results within the context of the client organization and in partnership with that organization (Ennis et al., 2005). Also essential is the ability to manage the coaching process from pre-coaching to contracting, assessment and goal setting, and transitioning to long-term development. Equally important skills include tailoring the coaching to the individual and organization, building and maintaining client relationships, creating and implementing a coaching development plan, and measuring the success of the coaching. Finally, you must be competent at applying the many coaching tools and techniques required to meet the varied needs of your diverse coaching clients and client organizations.

Consulting Practice Development and Management

Whether you are an internal or external executive coach, you must develop and manage your practice in a professional manner. The growing market of executive coaching requires you to establish your own unique value proposition to differentiate yourself in the marketplace or in your organization. You must then build your own capabilities and resources to succeed in your practice. There are eight key elements for you to develop and manage as a professional executive coach:

1. Your own education, training, supervision, and continued development in the knowledge, skills, and practice of executive coaching;
2. Strategic and marketing plans, whether you are an external or internal consultant;
3. Descriptions and marketing material for your coaching services targeted to your target markets;

4. A professional network for referrals to you as well as from you;
5. A toolbox of resources for meeting the needs of your clients, such as assessments, guides, readings, educational materials, and media;
6. An office infrastructure, including telecommunications, a scheduling system, and administrative support;
7. Research and publication; and
8. Community service.

The rest of this book is organized to help you build and manage these eight aspects of professional executive coaching.

TYPES OF EXECUTIVE COACHING

The goals of individual executive coaching projects are as varied as the individuals and organizations you serve. There are seven common areas of focus.

High-Potential Coaching — tie to org outcomes

High-potential individuals have not yet taken on significant leadership roles, but their organization has identified them as good prospects for future leadership or as part of a formal succession plan. Examples of coaching goals for high-potential individuals include:

- Making career decisions
- Developing basic management skills
- Refocusing from tactical management to more strategic leadership
- Refocusing from technical to managerial and leadership activities
- Identifying potential, strengths, and interests to match them with an appropriate development track

On-Boarding Coaching

Experienced leaders who have been or are about to be assigned to a new leadership role can benefit from on-boarding coaching. Goals for these individuals include:

- Facilitating an agreement between the coachee and key constituents on the charter for the assignment
- Building stakeholder relationships
- Developing an accelerated learning plan for leaders taking on new responsibilities (Betof & Harwood, 1992)

Continued Leadership-Development Coaching

Experienced managers and leaders often need to develop their leadership capabilities or expand their repertoires before taking on greater responsibility or more strategic leadership roles. Their coaching goals may include:

- Building executive presence
- Demonstrating greater passion to inspire the organization
- Driving a visionary strategic planning process
- Increasing collaboration with peers or a board on key strategic initiatives
- Building emotional intelligence competencies

Remedial Coaching

Leaders and managers may be having difficulty meeting their current responsibilities. Sometimes their leadership style prevents them from achieving needed results for the organization, or they accomplish short-term results in ways that are not aligned with the values, mission, vision, or strategy of the organization. These leaders need remedial coaching on such goals as:

- Stopping the overuse of independence or assertiveness that intimidates people

- Showing greater patience with people with different styles who need more time to think and plan
- Setting priorities and focusing on key objectives
- Holding people accountable and providing coaching when delegating responsibilities to others
- Acting in accordance with the law and the policies and procedures of the organization

Group or Team Coaching

With the support of a coach, small groups or teams of managers, leaders, and high-potential employees with similar development needs or shared goals learn to work together, coach each other, and build a support network for future collaboration. Their goals may include:

- Building partnerships with team members or cross-functional peers
- Developing coaching skills
- Gaining emotional intelligence in empathy and managing conflict
- Diversifying presentation style for different audiences
- Improving team dynamics
- Learning supervisory skills

Legacy Coaching

Leaders in later phases of their professional careers may want to prepare their successors, leave a legacy, transition to new roles, or identify activities to pursue in the next stage of life. Legacy coaching includes among its goals:

- Putting together a retirement or semiretirement activity portfolio
- Establishing a vision to inspire growth in the organization

- Planning a memoir that focuses on the leader's tenure at the organization
- Developing a transition plan for the senior executive who is taking over the reins

Targeted Coaching

An already strong leader may want to develop or refine a particular skill set, achieve a specific result, or work on a special project. Targeted coaching includes:

- Developing a project plan for a key initiative
- Improving influence skills
- "Managing up" to senior managers in the organization
- Working with the board of directors to build a mergers-and-acquisitions strategy with accompanying funding

EXECUTIVE COACHING CHECKLIST

On a very practical basis, professional executive coaches usually work in close partnership with the people they coach and key members of the coachee's organization. Here is a checklist of the typical steps a coach manages from beginning to end:

Before Coaching
- ☐ *Match-up:* Initial relationship building, sharing of needs and qualifications. Meet with representatives of the client organization to discuss the perceived needs for the coaching, your qualifications and approach, and the potential match between you and coaching needs. You and your coachee explore your styles, preferences, strengths, similarities, and differences to determine if you could work well together in a coaching relationship.
- ☐ *Coachability check:* You and the coachee determine if the time is right for coaching. Depending on career, life, and work situation, is the coachee motivated, available, and capable of getting the most from the coaching?

☐ *Contracting:* You, your firm, coachee, coachee's boss, human resources manager, or others in the coachee's organization agree, verbally and in writing, on the goals, ground rules, roles, process, time line, fees, and working relationships related to the coaching.

☐ *Initial goal setting:* Meet, separately and together, with the coachee, coachee's boss, the appropriate human resources professional, or others to identify and agree on general goals for the coaching. At this stage, goals may include building leadership skills, improving the performance of the coachee's direct reports, or accelerating the delivery of results for a critical project. These initial goals may change after the first phase of coaching, once data have been gathered and assessments completed to determine the coachee's developmental needs and the assistance necessary to achieve organizational results.

During Coaching
☐ Assessment, feedback, and development planning
☐ Specific goal setting and agreements on how to support the coaching
☐ Initial coaching sessions
☐ Progress check
☐ Continued coaching sessions

Ending Coaching
☐ Final progress check
☐ Long-term development plan
☐ Final coaching session
☐ Final meeting for closure and continued development and support

CHOOSING A COACH

Organizations employ coaches from both inside the organization and outside, and often a combination of both.

Internal Executive Coaches

Larger organizations and those more experienced with executive coaching often hire and develop professional coaches as employees. There are benefits to using internal coaches: they know the culture, people, and strategy of the organization and can provide support both formally, through an established process, and informally as the need arises. But internal coaches face certain challenges. Since they are part of the culture, they may lack the objectivity, willingness, or ability to challenge the status quo. Their livelihood and acceptance into their peer group, after all, depend on fitting into the organization and staying employed.

Other difficulties concern confidentiality and conflict of interest, when internal coaches push back on or give difficult feedback to senior executives who control employment and compensation. The insider can be viewed as just another person down the hall rather than an expert with great insights and expertise from working with leaders in other organizations. On the other hand, insiders can be of great help if they are considered role models of leadership and have proven skills coaching and mentoring in the organization.

Coaching is key in supervising and developing employees and colleagues. A manager often provides coaching not as a professional executive coach but as a leader skilled at helping others identify developmental opportunities, build capabilities, and achieve results through performance management and professional development activities. Such coaching often takes place within the supervisory relationship, but can also occur as part of the organization's performance management or mentoring process. If such a process exists, it is the best way for an employee to find an internal coach or mentor. Another way is to network with others to identify leaders who can help employees develop and advocate for their development and advancement.

THE HUMAN RESOURCES PROFESSIONAL AS AN EXECUTIVE COACH

Human resources professionals who serve as executive coaches in their organizations can achieve great success. Their roles and expectations for their coaching services must be clearly defined. Even the most qualified and supported internal coaches may find it difficult to coach senior-level executives except in unusual situations where trust is high, confidentiality is well defined, and policies and procedures exist to reassure employees that their coaching sessions will not come back to haunt them. When it is not the best option for internal human resources professionals to provide coaching, they can still play a critical role by helping leaders find coaches and support the coaching. Many organizations establish a pool of screened, recommended external coaches who can be matched to the individual and the situation for a coaching engagement. The human resources professional can partner with leaders, their bosses, and external coaches to manage and participate in the coaching process.

STRUCTURE OF AN EXECUTIVE COACHING SESSION

There are many styles of executive coaching. Depending on your stylistic tendencies, the activities of coaching can vary widely. Some styles are based on teaching and verbal dialogue. Others are more structured around solving problems, accomplishing work, rehearsing new behaviors, and practicing new skills. Still others treat the coaching session as a catalyst for learning and getting things done between the coaching sessions. Many coaches are eclectic in their approach, combining various styles and activities to tailor their coaching to the needs of each coachee. The following agenda for coaching sessions is very basic, focusing on a balance of different coaching styles and methods:

Agenda Topics for a Coaching Session
- *What's new?* The coachee updates you, as coach, on what has happened since you last met. Together you discuss implications for the coachee's role, priorities, activities, and what to focus on in coaching.
- *What has the coachee worked on and achieved since the previous coaching session?* The coachee reports on progress toward

goals, assignments, and activities associated with the coaching and how the learning from previous sessions has been applied on the job. This is your opportunity to reinforce learning, leadership competencies, new practices, and results. It is also an opportunity for further coaching to meet stated goals.

- *During this session, how can we work on current and future goals in the coaching plan?* This is the coachee's real-time work: learning and practicing new skills; trying, shaping, and changing work habits; building self-awareness and restructuring assumptions, beliefs, and ways of thinking that interfere with success; developing strategic plans; analyzing data and learning new ways to develop solutions to work on problems.

- *How can we plan for the next coaching sessions and upcoming activities?* Together, explore and agree on what the coachee will do to apply the learning from this session. Determine how you and others will support these activities. Then set the specific agenda for the next coaching session and agree on what each of you will do in preparation.

- *How can we continually improve the coaching as we move forward?* Debrief the coaching process with your coachee. To maximize both the process and its results, identify which strategies are working successfully and what should change. Explore ways to inform and involve the coachee's boss, board, and others who support the coaching.

Leadership Development Goals and Organizational Results of Executive Coaching

Over the past few decades, I have had the privilege of coaching hundreds of leaders and would-be leaders at just about every level in every function, industry, geographic region, and organizational situation. In each case, I have analyzed the findings from objective assessments and self-evaluations, plus feedback from the coachee's boards, superiors, peers, subordinates, customers, vendors, and others. I have identified the most frequent leadership development goals and organization results on which the executive coaching focused.

The following list is not all-inclusive, but rather an evidence-based, representative sample of many of the most common areas addressed in executive coaching:

Leadership Development Goals
- Appropriate sense of, and expression of, humor
- Assertiveness
- Collaboration
- Conflict management
- Customer management
- Decision making
- Delegation
- Demonstrating passion
- Emotional intelligence (awareness of and managing emotions and relationships for oneself and with others)
- Executive presence
- Giving positive and constructive feedback
- Hiring talent
- Influence
- Innovation
- Listening
- Managing one's own career
- Managing positive politics
- Managing up (to bosses and other superiors)
- Mentoring, coaching, and developing others' talents and careers
- Negotiation
- Performance management
- Presentation skills
- Problem solving
- Project management
- Strategic planning
- Stress management
- Tactical planning

- Team building
- Time management, setting priorities, and managing according to priorities
- Work-life balance

Organizational Results Goals
- Achieving more results with less effort
- Aligning with the board of directors
- Building a learning organization
- Building a talent pool for succession planning
- Building employee morale and loyalty
- Cutting costs
- Cutting product-development cycle time
- Developing a compelling organizational vision, mission, and strategy
- Diversifying sources of business and revenue
- Doing more with less resources
- Ensuring consistent compliance with ethical, legal, and professional guidelines
- Growing the organization
- Improving customer satisfaction, loyalty, and retention
- Improving investor relations
- Improving organizational communication
- Improving quality
- Increasing cross-divisional/functional cooperation
- Increasing organizational efficiency
- Increasing productivity
- Increasing revenue
- Increasing the success rate of newly appointed leaders and key players
- Maintaining organizational stability during significant change
- Reducing turnover in human resources
- Restructuring the organization
- Seeking and achieving successful mergers and acquisitions

Is Executive Coaching Right for You?

Whether you are already practicing executive coaching or are considering the field for the future, the following questions can help you decide if your needs, interests, abilities, and tendencies are a good match with professional executive coaching.

The more you answer each question positively and with confidence, the more executive coaching may be right for you. Chapter 2 will help you assess your knowledge and expertise and begin to use your strengths to build your practice.

Your Needs
- Is it important for you to change people's lives: both the leaders you coach and the people they lead and interact with?
- Do you care about the success of organizations, their business results, and their return to key constituents?
- Are your income needs aligned with executive coaching fees? Are you prepared to provide significant coaching services for lower fees as a contribution to the mission or purpose of the organizations you will serve?

Your Interests
- Are you fascinated by leadership, organizational systems, and the intensity of the leader's role in organizations?
- Do you like to deal with high-pressure situations in which major organizational issues and key work relationships are dealt with openly and practically?
- Do you enjoy working one-on-one and in small groups with smart people? Do you have a deep desire to learn continually as you help others learn, change what they do, build their skills, and work more effectively?

Your Abilities
- Do you have mature self-confidence, humility, assertiveness, openness, and flexibility in what you do and how you do it?
- Do you have a reserve of positive energy, optimism, and resilience?

- Do you process information quickly, envision scenarios, understand how you and how others think and feel, and build and manage relationships easily?

Your Tendencies
- Are you comfortable being independent while still collaborating with others to support shared goals?
- Are you geared to use data and evidence to help people make decisions?
- Do you have an action orientation to solving problems, capitalizing on opportunities, and getting things done?

FINDING CLIENTS BEST SUITED FOR YOU

Each executive coach is best suited to serve certain clients with specific needs and styles in certain industries and kinds of organizations. Before hanging out your shingle, determine what type of client to seek.

Marketing Yourself

Chapters 3 and 4 will help you decide what you have to offer as an executive coach, whom you can best serve with your unique value proposition, and how to build and market your practice to attract and retain the right clients for you. Those chapters are based on five assumptions about marketing yourself as an executive coach:

1. You can't attract the right clients before you decide what type of client you want to serve.
2. You can't decide which clients you want to serve before deciding what differentiates you in the market and how to build on your strengths and goals to achieve personal, professional, and business success.
3. You can't decide on your value proposition and the goals for your practice before you are truly aware of who you are, what you care about, what you want to achieve, and what is realistic as a practice in your target market.

4. As a professional executive coach, the most important building block of your practice is you. You need to know your strengths and development needs to position your practice, fill and compensate for gaps in knowledge and skills, and use your attributes and abilities. Chapter 2 of this book will help you to complete that self-assessment.

5. Finally, you don't sell executive coaching like you sell cars. As a professional, relationship-oriented service, people select you as a coach because someone they trust has recommended you or you build trust and respect quickly when you first meet with potential coaching clients. To accomplish that, you must demonstrate that you understand their situation and will succeed in developing them as leaders and achieving organizational results.

Getting Selected as the Right Executive Coach

Once you identify your target market, follow four steps to convince organizations and their leaders to select you as a coach. These steps are applicable for both the external coach and the internal human resources or organization development professional:

1. Make yourself known in the market.
2. Stand out from the competition.
3. Develop referral sources so potential coachees and the people who find coaches for them will contact you when the need arises.
4. Serve your clients and potential clients extraordinarily well—they will recommend you to others and turn to you again.

This Book Will Help You Build and Manage Your Executive Coaching Practice

This chapter has provided a framework for executive coaching. Now turn to Chapter 2 for your executive coaching self-assessment. It will help you identify your strengths, knowledge and skills to develop, and attributes and abilities to use or compensate for in your practice.

With Chapter 3 you'll begin building and marketing your executive coaching value proposition. You'll decide what you want to accomplish through your practice, target the market and types of clients you can best serve, and begin to develop a step-by-step plan for establishing your practice.

Chapter 4 is your guide to building and managing a professional executive coaching practice. You will learn about referral and resource networks, a coaching toolbox, office infrastructure, coaching project-management systems, professional and peer supervision, research and publication, and community service.

Are you transitioning from a specialty in mental health, business management, management and organization-development consulting, personal/life coaching, human resource management, or another area of coaching? Chapter 5 will help you manage the transition to executive coaching.

Chapter 6 helps you put it all together and build your professional executive coaching practice plan. We focus on the form your practice will take, your professional development plan, a marketing plan, the building blocks of your practice, a management plan, and a transition plan from your current area of work.

The Appendix provides practical resources for building and managing your professional executive coaching practice: a bibliography of useful readings, Web-based resources, tools and materials, professional organizations, and other sources.

Executive coaching is an exciting and challenging field. As a professional discipline, it is just beginning to define itself and establish professional standards. If you are prepared to learn continually, work hard, and build a practice on a foundation of knowledge, skills, tools, and useful and practical service, executive coaching will reward you amply. Best of luck as you use this book and continue on your path into the field of professional executive coaching.

CHAPTER TWO

Assessing Your Competencies as a Professional Executive Coach

As you begin to build your practice as a professional executive coach, what is first on your list? It's not the name of your practice or a brochure about your services. It's not even sources for business referrals. It's you.

An executive coach is like an athlete or surgeon. If you decide to play professional baseball, you'll begin by determining if you have what it takes to make the cut. You'll focus on the position you will play. And you'll get feedback. If you don't know what you're good at, you won't be able to make the most of your strengths and correct your weaknesses. You can compete and perform to your potential only by developing self-awareness, using your strengths, and improving continuously. The same goes for eye surgery: first you study medicine, then specialize in ophthalmology, and finally perfect your surgical skills. Professional executive coaches must go through a similar process of general to specialized training and development.

People who contact me wanting to enter the field of executive coaching often describe themselves as "good listeners," "good at solving problems," and "intrigued by how businesses operate." Many training programs in executive coaching focus on techniques instead of the strong base of knowledge required to apply those techniques correctly. If you develop the needed knowledge and techniques, you will still need to compensate for any attributes or lack of ability that could impede your progress. By focusing on all of these competencies, you can develop a plan to maximize your success as a professional executive coach.

This chapter includes the following tools to help you get started:

- Self-assessment of core competencies for professional executive coaches
- 360-degree feedback survey
- Your professional development plan
- Executive coaching professional development strategies

CORE COMPETENCIES FOR EXECUTIVE COACHES

You'll begin with a self-assessment on a set of core competencies identified by the board of the Executive Coaching Forum, of which I was a founder and chairman. This group of experts, from varied backgrounds and perspectives, gathered input and feedback from many other professionals and collaborated with an expert in competency model development. Drawing on our own experiences as executive coaches, managers of coaching in organizations, and coaching researchers and educators, we documented the competencies, skills, attributes, and abilities we observed in the best executive coaches. If you lack these competencies, it will be difficult for you to succeed.

Ultimately we identified four competency areas for the executive coach. We agreed that few coaches are highly effective in every single competency, and that certain coaching engagements demand more expertise in specific skill sets. In our experience, however, significant competence in each of these four areas is important for executive coaches:

1. Psychological knowledge;
2. Business acumen;
3. Organizational knowledge; and
4. Coaching knowledge, tasks, and skills.

For four years, I worked with my colleagues from the Massachusetts School of Professional Psychology and the Graduate School Alliance for Executive Coaching to test the first four competency areas in the development and education of graduate school curricula. Our graduate students voiced and demonstrated the need for a set of knowledge and skills associated with building and managing a professional coaching practice. I have added this area of competence to this chapter's self-assessment:

5. Consulting practice development and management.

The Executive Coaching Forum's competency model also incorporated a set of personal attributes and abilities important to helping executive coaches succeed. Many of these personal qualities are related to the competency of "emotional intelligence" repeatedly demonstrated as important for successful leaders in organizational settings (Chernis & Goleman, 2001). These attributes and abilities are addressed in the final area of the Executive Coach Self-Assessment.

In addition to the self-assessment, a 360-degree survey is included. The survey has two uses: to obtain feedback about yourself from others and to evaluate someone else's competence or potential as an executive coach. People who know you well in the executive coaching context can provide you with useful feedback on your knowledge, skills, attributes, and abilities.

Neither the self-assessment nor the 360-degree survey is a validated instrument. They have not been researched to establish normative databases of competent executive coaches against which to compare yourself or others. Rather, the surveys will help you gain greater awareness of a set of core coaching competencies identified by a group of experts, and to pinpoint potential areas in which you or others could benefit from further professional development.

Self-Assessment: Core Competencies for Professional Executive Coaches

Please rate yourself on the degree to which each of the following statements is true for you today. If you are an executive coach, rate your current competencies. If you are new to the field, rate your ability or attributes to be able to coach executives.

To get the most from the survey, be as honest as you can with your ratings:

Rating Scale

4 = Strong working knowledge
3 = Moderate working knowledge
2 = Not much working knowledge
1 = Little or no working knowledge

Your name: _____

Today's date: _____

Knowledge Areas

Categories

1. Psychological knowledge
2. Business acumen
3. Organizational knowledge
4. Coaching knowledge

1. PSYCHOLOGICAL KNOWLEDGE

To what degree do you have a working knowledge of each of the following?

Much of this self-assessment is based on *Core Competencies of the Executive Coach*, Version 2005.1, developed by The Executive Coaching Forum, © 2005. All Rights Reserved. Permission for its use in building this self-assessment and the 360-degree feedback survey was granted by the model's authors.

Rating Scale
4 = Strong working knowledge
3 = Moderate working knowledge
2 = Not much working knowledge
1 = Little or no working knowledge

Psychological Knowledge Area	Rating
1. Personality theories	
2. Models of human motivation	
3. Adult development theories, including moral, intellectual, emotional, relational, and spiritual development	
4. Models of adult learning	
5. Models of career development	
6. Models of personal and behavioral change	
7. Work/life balance	
8. Stress management techniques	
9. Social psychology and how social factors impact individual and group behavior	
10. How to identify individuals in need of psychological or medical referral	
11. Models of emotional intelligence	
12. The role of gender differences in adulthood	
13. Models and methods of 360-degree feedback	
14. Models of personal and leadership style (e.g., MBTI, DISC)	

2. BUSINESS ACUMEN

To what degree do you have a working knowledge of each of the following?

Rating Scale
4 = Strong working knowledge
3 = Moderate working knowledge
2 = Not much working knowledge
1 = Little or no working knowledge

	BUSINESS ACUMEN KNOWLEDGE AREA	RATING
1.	Basic business practices and concepts	
2.	Basic financial concepts (e.g., income and balance sheets)	
3.	Business functions and their interdependencies	
4.	The strategic planning process and its relationship with team and individual goal setting	
5.	Current information technologies	
6.	The role of information technology in business (e.g., ERP, enterprise management)	
7.	Process improvement technologies	
8.	Global capitalism and global firms	
9.	The differences between regulated and nonregulated businesses	
10.	The differences between for-profit and not-for-profit businesses	

11.	The key leadership roles in organizations (e.g., COO, CFO, CTO, CEO, Executive Director, Board Chair)	
12.	Knowledge of current business events, issues, and trends	
13.	Management principles and processes	
14.	Human resource management programs and processes	
15.	The appropriate use of communication technologies	

3. ORGANIZATIONAL KNOWLEDGE

To what degree do you have a working knowledge of each of the following?

Rating Scale
4 = Strong working knowledge
3 = Moderate working knowledge
2 = Not much working knowledge
1 = Little or no working knowledge

ORGANIZATIONAL KNOWLEDGE AREA	RATING
1. Basic organizational structures, systems, and processes including functional, divisional, and matrix organizational forms as well as the behavioral patterns associated with each	
2. Organizational assessment and diagnosis	
3. Organizational design and development principles and practices	

4. The impact and role of organizational cultures and subcultures	
5. The phases of team development and the characteristics of effective team leadership	
6. Models of leadership	
7. Leadership development programs and processes	
8. Organization development methodologies	
9. Organizational systems theory	
10. The nature and role of organizational politics, power, and influence	
11. Organizational change management theories and practices	
12. Consulting theory and practices	
13. The role of ethics in business and in organizational consulting	
14. Models of the learning organization	
15. Models of succession and leadership transition	

4. COACHING KNOWLEDGE

To what degree do you have a working knowledge of each of the following?

Rating Scale
4 = Strong working knowledge
3 = Moderate working knowledge
2 = Not much working knowledge
1 = Little or no working knowledge

Core Competencies for Executive Coaches

Coaching Knowledge Area	Rating
1. The history of executive coaching	
2. Executive coaching models and theories	
3. The definitions of coaching and executive coaching as a specialty practice	
4. Seven overarching principles for executive coaching: systems perspective, results orientation, business focus, partnership, competence, integrity, and judgment	
5. Seven guidelines for practicing the different phases of executive coaching by the coach, the executive, and the executive's organization: managing confidentiality, pre-coaching activities, contracting, assessment, goal setting, coaching, and transitioning to long-term development	
6. The underlying principles and approaches of the different types of coaching and how they differ from and/or can be incorporated into executive coaching	
7. The distinction between executive coaching and other models of coaching	
8. The role of manager as coach and the impact of executive coaching on the development of that capability	
9. The roles coaches can play and when and how to effectively apply them (e.g., trainer, mentor, advisor)	

10. The differences between executive coaching and other helping methods for executives (e.g., counseling, consulting, therapy, mentoring)	
11. How coaching theories and methods apply to various situations of individual coaching clients	
12. How to tailor the coaching process to adapt it to the unique needs and circumstances of the coachee and the organization	
13. Measurement of coaching outcomes and process	
14. Research findings on executive coaching (past and emerging)	
15. The core competencies of executive coaches	
16. The wide variety of available coaching resources (books, articles, Internet sites, tools, etc.)	
17. How to maintain and implement a continuous plan for your own professional development	

Comments on your knowledge areas:

_____

_____

_____

Executive Coaching Tasks And Skills

Categories
1. Building and maintaining coaching relationships
2. Contracting
3. Assessment
4. Development planning
5. Facilitating development and change
6. Ending the formal coaching and transitioning to long-term development
7. Building and managing a professional executive coaching practice

1. Building and Maintaining Coaching Relationships

To what degree are you currently capable of doing the following as an executive coach?

Rating Scale
4 = Very capable
3 = Moderately capable
2 = Somewhat capable
1 = Hardly capable or not capable at all

Building and Maintaining Coaching Relationships Task/Skill Area	Rating
1. Build and sustain trust	
2. Hold the coachee, his/her boss, and Human Resources (HR) accountable to the coaching agreements	
3. Identify and manage resistance and conflict	
4. Influence with and without authority	
5. Maintain confidentiality on sensitive organizational and individual issues	

6. Hold multiple perspectives	
7. Solicit feedback on your own performance as coach	
8. Utilize the coaching relationship as a tool to help the coachee	
9. Maintain the balance of the close coaching relationship and professional boundaries	
10. Make and explain observations about what goes on in the coaching relationship and its similarities and differences to the coachee's other relationships	
11. Appropriately challenge	

2. CONTRACTING

To what degree are you currently capable of doing the following as an executive coach?

Rating Scale
4 = Very capable
3 = Moderately capable
2 = Somewhat capable
1 = Hardly capable or not capable at all

CONTRACTING TASK/SKILL AREA	RATING
1. Evaluate the readiness of the coachee for coaching	
2. Engage all appropriate constituents in goal setting and agenda setting for the coaching (coachee, boss, HR, others)	

3. Obtain commitment and support from all appropriate constituents	
4. Establish guidelines for confidentiality	
5. Establish the boss's and HR's role in the coaching	
6. Facilitate agenda-setting and goal-setting meetings between the coachee, his/her boss, and the HR professional	
7. Develop realistic and challenging coaching goals	
8. Set realistic time frames for accomplishing the coaching goals	
9. Re-contract when appropriate	
10. Tailor the coaching process to the unique needs of the coachee and organization	

3. ASSESSMENT

To what degree are you currently capable of doing the following as an executive coach?

Rating Scale
4 = Very capable
3 = Moderately capable
2 = Somewhat capable
1 = Hardly capable or not capable at all

ASSESSMENT TASK/SKILL AREA	RATING
1. Design assessment plans	
2. Administer and interpret 360-degree feedback instruments and measures of personal and leadership style (e.g., MBTI, DISC)	
3. Interview the coachee and his/her key constituents	
4. Unobtrusively observe/shadow coachees in their work environment	
5. Gather data from multiple sources, aggregate the data, and present the results and implications in a useful format	
6. Use the results of assessment tools and instruments to evaluate the coachee's strengths, weaknesses, abilities, tendencies, preferences, behavior patterns, emotions, thinking styles, opportunities, constraints, and other factors important to the coaching	
7. Use the results of assessment tools, instruments, and other methods to evaluate the coachee's organizational context (e.g., organizational characteristics, strengths, weaknesses, opportunities, constraints)	
8. Refer when appropriate to employee assistance programs, career counselors, or other specialists for the administration, scoring, and interpreting of assessments	
9. Identify the coachee's learning style	

4. DEVELOPMENT PLANNING

To what degree are you currently capable of doing the following as an executive coach?

Rating Scale
4 = Very capable
3 = Moderately capable
2 = Somewhat capable
1 = Hardly capable or not capable at all

	DEVELOPMENT PLANNING TASK/SKILL AREA	RATING
1.	Partner with Human Resources	
2.	Conduct debriefing and feedback sessions with the coachee regarding the assessments and 360-degree results	
3.	Establish specific coaching goals (behavioral, cognitive, skills, business, relationships, etc.)	
4.	Help the coachee design and create action plans and a coaching timetable	
5.	Help the coachee, his/her boss, and HR to review assessment results within agreed-on guidelines for confidentiality and translate those results into actionable coaching strategies	
6.	Establish qualitative and quantitative measures of results for the coaching goals	
7.	Determine what can be achieved in coaching and recommend appropriate training and other methods to achieve other developmental goals	

8. Quickly identify the need for, and make referrals to, other helping professionals	
9. Gain commitment for the coachee's self-management of coaching action plans	
10. Help the boss to provide useful feedback and to coach the coachee as his/her manager	

5. FACILITATING DEVELOPMENT AND CHANGE

To what degree are you currently capable of doing the following as an executive coach?

Rating Scale
4 = Very capable
3 = Moderately capable
2 = Somewhat capable
1 = Hardly capable or not capable at all

FACILITATING DEVELOPMENT AND CHANGE TASK/SKILL AREA	RATING
1. Take the coachee's point of view and offer alternative points of view	
2. Show accurate empathy	
3. Listen actively and respectfully	
4. Communicate clearly, concisely, and directly	
5. Provide constructive feedback	
6. Observe the coachee's behavior in coaching sessions and provide real-time feedback	
7. Offer specific strategies and suggested behavior changes	

8. Demonstrate and serve as a role model in the coaching for new work methods and ways of communicating	
9. Create and raise awareness	
10. Design assignments that encourage experimentation, reflection, and learning	
11. Ask powerful questions	
12. Support and confront appropriately	
13. Challenge assumptions	
14. Solicit solutions	
15. Swiftly translate ideas into action plans	
16. Develop management, executive, and leadership skills	
17. Provide learning resources as needed (reading, models, etc.)	
18. Involve the boss as the ongoing coach	
19. Measure and monitor the coaching process and results	
20. Address new issues and learning opportunities as they arise	
21. Be aware of and recognize your own part as the coach in the coachee's problem or situation through various methods (e.g., peer supervision, consultation)	
22. Coach the boss to better support the coachee and his/her business and coaching objectives	

6. ENDING FORMAL COACHING AND TRANSITIONING TO LONG-TERM DEVELOPMENT

To what degree are you currently capable of doing the following as an executive coach?

Rating Scale
4 = Very capable
3 = Moderately capable
2 = Somewhat capable
1 = Hardly capable or not capable at all

	ENDING FORMAL COACHING AND TRANSISTIONING TO LONG-TERM DEVELOPMENT TASK/SKILL AREA	RATING
1.	Identify the appropriate ending point in the formal coaching process	
2.	Initiate discussion with the coachee, his/her manager, and others in the organization about bringing the formal coaching to an end	
3.	Work with the coachee to identify ongoing developmental supports and resources in his/her environment and to establish a transition/ending plan	
4.	Work with the coachee to establish postcoaching developmental goals and a plan for meeting those goals	
5.	Work toward and encourage the coachee's independence	
6.	Encourage the coachee to continue learning on his/her own	

7. Conduct formal ending meeting with the coachee, his/her manager, and Human Resources	
8. Leave the possibility open for future coaching as the need arises and within the guidelines of the coaching contract	

7. BUILDING AND MANAGING A PROFESSIONAL EXECUTIVE COACHING PRACTICE

To what degree are you currently capable of doing the following as an executive coach?

Rating Scale
4 = Very capable
3 = Moderately capable
2 = Somewhat capable
1 = Hardly capable or not capable at all

BUILDING AND MANAGING A PROFESSIONAL EXECUTIVE COACHING PRACTICE TASK/SKILL AREA	RATING
1. Managing your own education, training, supervision, and continued development in the knowledge, skills, and practice of executive coaching	
2. Building your marketing plan (as an external or internal consultant)	
3. Developing descriptions/marketing material on your coaching services and vehicles to get that information to your target market	

4. Building and managing your professional network for referrals to you and from you	
5. Building and maintaining your toolbox of resources from which you can draw to address the needs of your varied clients (assessments, guides, readings, educational materials, media, etc.)	
6. Building and managing your "office" infrastructure (telecommunications, scheduling system, administrative support, etc.)	
7. Building and maintaining your practice management systems (client management, business and financial management, communications, quality, research, publishing, community service, etc.)	

Comments on your executive coaching tasks and skills:

_____
_____
_____
_____

GENERAL ATTRIBUTES AND ABILITIES

Categories
1. Mature self-confidence
2. Positive energy
3. Assertiveness
4. Interpersonal sensitivity
5. Openness and flexibility
6. Goal orientation

7. Partnering and influence
8. Continuous learning and development
9. Integrity

1. MATURE SELF-CONFIDENCE

To what degree do you demonstrate the following attributes and abilities?

Rating Scale

4 = A great deal
3 = Quite a bit
2 = Somewhat
1 = Hardly or not at all

MATURE SELF-CONFIDENCE ATTRIBUTE OR ABILITY	RATING
1. Appear comfortable with yourself	
2. Show maturity; demonstrate that you have gained wisdom from personal and professional experience	
3. Show confidence; place an appropriate value on your own abilities and perspectives	
4. Show humility; demonstrate awareness that success usually follows from the efforts of a group or team of other individuals, not solely from your own efforts	

2. POSITIVE ENERGY

To what degree do you demonstrate the following attributes and abilities?

Rating Scale
4 = A great deal
3 = Quite a bit
2 = Somewhat
1 = Hardly or not at all

POSITIVE ENERGY ATTRIBUTE OR ABILITY	RATING
1. Show energy, optimism, and enthusiasm	
2. Effectively manage your emotions	
3. Demonstrate resilience; bounce back after mistakes and failures	
4. Demonstrate an appropriate sense of humor	
5. Help the coachee to appreciate his/her strengths and ability to overcome barriers	
6. Help the coachee to imagine new possibilities	
7. Convey hopefulness	

3. ASSERTIVENESS

To what degree do you demonstrate the following attributes and abilities?

Rating Scale
4 = A great deal
3 = Quite a bit
2 = Somewhat
1 = Hardly or not at all

Assertiveness Attribute or Ability	Rating
1. Assert yourself and appropriately say "no" to set limits	
2. Confront coachees and others who are not following through on commitments	
3. Speak directly with others even when discussing difficult or sensitive issues	
4. Address conflict with others directly and constructively	
5. Communicate in ways that reflect respect for your own worth and the worth of others	

4. Interpersonal Sensitivity

To what degree do you demonstrate the following attributes and abilities?

Rating Scale
4 = A great deal
3 = Quite a bit
2 = Somewhat
1 = Hardly or not at all

Interpersonal Sensitivity Attribute or Ability	Rating
1. Show empathy with others	
2. Are sensitive to how your style impacts others or fits with the needs of others	
3. Demonstrate an interest in people; show curiosity about the lives, goals, experiences, and perspectives of others	

4. Show compassion and demonstrate concern for the needs and emotional well-being of others	
5. Demonstrate tact; give difficult or critical information to others in a respectful and supportive fashion	
6. Learn and remember other people's most important concerns	
7. Use active listening techniques (e.g., maintaining full attention, periodically summarizing, being nonjudgmental) to reflect and acknowledge other people's feelings and concerns	

5. Openness and Flexibility

To what degree do you demonstrate the following attributes and abilities?

Rating Scale
4 = A great deal
3 = Quite a bit
2 = Somewhat
1 = Hardly or not at all

Openness and Flexibility Attribute or Ability	Rating
1. Are able to understand and appreciate perspectives that differ from your own	
2. Tailor your own approach to fit the preferences and needs of the coachee	

3. Demonstrate flexibility; change course or approach when the situation demands it	
4. Understand and relate to individuals and groups from a variety of cultures with values different from your own culture	
5. Seek out and use feedback to enhance the coaching engagement	

6. GOAL ORIENTATION

To what degree do you demonstrate the following attributes and abilities?

Rating Scale
4 = A great deal
3 = Quite a bit
2 = Somewhat
1 = Hardly or not at all

GOAL ORIENTATION ATTRIBUTE OR ABILITY	RATING
1. Set challenging but achievable goals for yourself	
2. Help coachees to identify and set realistic and challenging goals	
3. Are highly motivated toward the pursuit of your goals	
4. Show resourcefulness; seek out, or help others seek out solutions under difficult or challenging conditions	
5. Demonstrate stability; stay on tasks for extended periods of time	

6. Show persistence; do not give up when faced with a challenge	
7. Demonstrate the ability to organize work; effectively plan and manage resources and time when pursuing a goal	

7. PARTNERING AND INFLUENCE

To what degree do you demonstrate the following attributes and abilities?

Rating Scale
4 = A great deal
3 = Quite a bit
2 = Somewhat
1 = Hardly or not at all

PARTNERING AND INFLUENCE ATTRIBUTE OR ABILITY	RATING
1. Carefully plan and tailor your own words in ways that achieve the desired impact	
2. Present arguments that address others' most important concerns and issues	
3. Involve others as partners in a process to gain their support and buy-in	
4. Show interest in and comfort with the context in which the coaching is taking place (for-profits, not-for-profits, health-care organizations, the public sector, marketing, finance, sales, R&D, etc.)	

5. Share some of the values of people in the organization in which the coaching is taking place; have a fundamental comfort with private enterprise and/or public endeavors	
6. Demonstrate inclusiveness by encouraging the participation of multiple stakeholders	

8. CONTINUOUS LEARNING AND DEVELOPMENT

To what degree do you demonstrate the following attributes and abilities?

Rating Scale
4 = A great deal
3 = Quite a bit
2 = Somewhat
1 = Hardly or not at all

CONTINUOUS LEARNING AND DEVELOPMENT ATTRIBUTE OR ABILITY	RATING
1. Seek feedback to enhance overall coaching effectiveness	
2. Assess and address gaps in your own knowledge and skill	
3. Undertake study and learning to enhance skills that will contribute to the coaching you provide	

9. INTEGRITY

To what degree do you demonstrate the following attributes and abilities?

Rating Scale
4 = A great deal
3 = Quite a bit

2 = Somewhat
1 = Hardly or not at all

INTEGRITY ATTRIBUTE/ABILITY	RATING
1. Take and hold an ethical stand regardless of financial or other pressures	
2. Carefully maintain appropriate confidentiality in all dealings	
3. Determine what is appropriate through careful contracting in your coaching and consulting relationships, with the goal of meeting the needs of all stakeholders	
4. Demonstrate personal integrity; "walk the talk"	
5. Appear genuine, honest, and straightforward regarding your agenda and needs	
6. Focus on and put the client's needs ahead of your own	
7. Make and keep commitments to others	
8. Avoid a coaching workload that compromises the quality of the coaching service	
9. Respect the established relationships between the client and other providers of coaching, consulting, and/or other services	

Comments on your general attributes and abilities:

_____

_____

_____

_____

Professional Executive Coach:
360-Degree Feedback Survey

Please rate the following person on the degree to which they have the knowledge, conduct the tasks, and demonstrate the skills, attributes, and abilities to be able to coach executives today.

If you do not understand the intended meaning of an item or don't think you know enough about the person to answer a specific item or section, just leave it blank. Otherwise, please be as honest as you can with your ratings to allow the person to get the most from the survey. Thank you.

The person about whom you are completing this survey:

_____

Today's date: _____

KNOWLEDGE AREAS

Categories
1. Psychological knowledge
2. Business acumen
3. Organizational knowledge
4. Coaching knowledge

1. PSYCHOLOGICAL KNOWLEDGE

To what degree does this person have a working knowledge of each of the following?

Like the self-assessment, the 360-degree feedback survey is based on *Core Competencies of the Executive Coach*, Version 2005.1, developed by The Executive Coaching Forum, © 2005. All Rights Reserved. Permission for its use in building this self-assessment and the 360-degree feedback survey was granted by the model's authors.

Rating Scale
4 = Strong working knowledge
3 = Moderate working knowledge
2 = Not much working knowledge
1 = Little or no working knowledge

PSYCHOLOGICAL KNOWLEDGE AREA	RATING
1. Personality theories	
2. Models of human motivation	
3. Adult development theories, including moral, intellectual, emotional, relational, and spiritual development	
4. Models of adult learning	
5. Models of career development	
6. Models of personal and behavioral change	
7. Work/life balance	
8. Stress management techniques	
9. Social psychology and how social factors impact individual and group behavior	
10. How to identify individuals in need of psychological or medical referral	
11. Models of emotional intelligence	
12. The role of gender differences in adulthood	
13. Models and methods of 360-degree feedback	
14. Models of personal and leadership style (e.g., MBTI, DISC)	

2. BUSINESS ACUMEN

To what degree does this person have a working knowledge of each of the following?

Rating Scale
4 = Strong working knowledge
3 = Moderate working knowledge
2 = Not much working knowledge
1 = Little or no working knowledge

BUSINESS ACUMEN KNOWLEDGE AREA	RATING
1. Basic business practices and concepts	
2. Basic financial concepts (e.g., income and balance sheets)	
3. Business functions and their interdependencies	
4. The strategic planning process and its relationship with team and individual goal setting	
5. Current information technologies	
6. The role of information technology in business (e.g., ERP, enterprise management)	
7. Process improvement technologies	
8. Global capitalism and global firms	
9. The differences between regulated and nonregulated businesses	
10. The differences between for-profit and not-for-profit businesses	

11.	The key leadership roles in organizations (e.g., COO, CFO, CTO, CEO, Executive Director, Board Chair)	
12.	Knowledge of current business events, issues, and trends	
13.	Management principles and processes	
14.	Human resource management programs and processes	
15.	The appropriate use of communication technologies	

3. ORGANIZATIONAL KNOWLEDGE

To what degree does this person have a working knowledge of each of the following?

Rating Scale
4 = Strong working knowledge
3 = Moderate working knowledge
2 = Not much working knowledge
1 = Little or no working knowledge

ORGANIZATIONAL KNOWLEDGE AREA	RATING
1. Basic organizational structures, systems, and processes including functional, divisional, and matrix organizational forms as well as the behavioral patterns associated with each	
2. Organizational assessment and diagnosis	
3. Organizational design and development principles and practices	

4. The impact and role of organizational cultures and subcultures	
5. The phases of team development and the characteristics of effective team leadership	
6. Models of leadership	
7. Leadership development programs and processes	
8. Organization development methodologies	
9. Organizational systems theory	
10. The nature and role of organizational politics, power, and influence	
11. Organizational change management theories and practices	
12. Consulting theory and practices	
13. The role of ethics in business and in organizational consulting	
14. Models of the learning organization	
15. Models of succession and leadership transition	

4. COACHING KNOWLEDGE

To what degree does this person have a working knowledge of each of the following?

Rating Scale
4 = Strong working knowledge
3 = Moderate working knowledge
2 = Not much working knowledge
1 = Little or no working knowledge

COACHING KNOWLEDGE AREA	RATING
1. The history of executive coaching	
2. Executive coaching models and theories	
3. The definitions of coaching and executive coaching as a specialty practice	
4. Seven overarching principles for executive coaching: systems perspective, results orientation, business focus, partnership, competence, integrity, and judgment	
5. Seven guidelines for practicing the different phases of executive coaching by the coach, the executive, and the executive's organization: managing confidentiality, pre-coaching activities, contracting, assessment, goal setting, coaching, and transitioning to long-term development	
6. The underlying principles and approaches of the different types of coaching and how they differ from and/or can be incorporated into executive coaching	
7. The distinction between executive coaching and other models of coaching	
8. The role of manager as coach and the impact of executive coaching on the development of that capability	
9. The roles coaches can play and when and how to effectively apply them (e.g., trainer, mentor, advisor)	

10.	The differences between executive coaching and other helping methods for executives (e.g., counseling, consulting, therapy, mentoring)	
11.	How coaching theories and methods apply to various situations of individual coaching clients	
12.	How to tailor the coaching process to adapt it to the unique needs and circumstances of the coachee and the organization	
13.	Measurement of coaching outcomes and process	
14.	Research findings on executive coaching (past and emerging)	
15.	The core competencies of executive coaches	
16.	The wide variety of available coaching resources (books, articles, Internet sites, tools, etc.)	
17.	How to maintain and implement a continuous plan for one's own professional development	

Comments on knowledge areas:

_____

_____

_____

_____

EXECUTIVE COACHING TASKS AND SKILLS

Categories
1. Building and maintaining coaching relationships
2. Contracting
3. Assessment
4. Development planning
5. Facilitating development and change
6. Ending formal coaching and transitioning to long-term development

1. BUILDING AND MAINTAINING COACHING RELATIONSHIPS

To what degree is this person currently capable of doing the following as an executive coach?

Rating Scale
4 = Very capable
3 = Moderately capable
2 = Somewhat capable
1 = Hardly capable or not capable at all

BUILDING AND MAINTAINING COACHING RELATIONSHIPS TASK/SKILL AREA	RATING
1. Build and sustain trust	
2. Hold the coachee, his/her boss, and HR accountable to the coaching agreements	
3. Identify and manage resistance and conflict	
4. Influence with and without authority	
5. Maintain confidentiality on sensitive organizational and individual issues	
6. Hold multiple perspectives	

7. Solicit feedback on one's own performance as coach	
8. Utilize the coaching relationship as a tool to help the coachee	
9. Maintain the balance of the close coaching relationship and professional boundaries	
10. Make and explain observations about what goes on in the coaching relationship and its similarities and differences to the coachee's other relationships	
11. Appropriately challenge	

2. CONTRACTING

To what degree is this person currently capable of doing the following as an executive coach?

Rating Scale
4 = Very capable
3 = Moderately capable
2 = Somewhat capable
1 = Hardly capable or not capable at all

CONTRACTING TASK/SKILL AREA	RATING
1. Evaluate the readiness of the coachee for coaching	
2. Engage all appropriate constituents in goal setting and agenda setting for the coaching (coachee, boss, HR, others)	
3. Obtain commitment and support from all appropriate constituents	

4. Establish guidelines for confidentiality	
5. Establish the boss's and HR's role in the coaching	
6. Facilitate agenda-setting and goal-setting meetings between the coachee, his/her boss, and the HR professional	
7. Develop realistic and challenging coaching goals	
8. Set realistic time frames for accomplishing the coaching goals	
9. Recontract when appropriate	
10. Tailor the coaching process to the unique needs of the coachee and organization	

3. ASSESSMENT

To what degree is this person currently capable of doing the following as an executive coach?

Rating Scale
4 = Very capable
3 = Moderately capable
2 = Somewhat capable
1 = Hardly capable or not capable at all

ASSESSMENT TASK/SKILL AREA	RATING
1. Design assessment plans	
2. Administer and interpret 360-degree feedback instruments and measures of personal and leadership style (e.g., MBTI, DISC)	

3. Interview the coachee and his/her key constituents	
4. Unobtrusively observe/shadow coachees in their work environment	
5. Gather data from multiple sources, aggregate the data, and present the results and implications in a useful format	
6. Use the results of assessment tools and instruments to evaluate the coachee's strengths, weaknesses, abilities, tendencies, preferences, behavior patterns, emotions, thinking styles, opportunities, constraints, and other factors important to the coaching	
7. Use the results of assessment tools, instruments, and other methods to evaluate the coachee's organizational context (e.g., organizational characteristics, strengths, weaknesses, opportunities, constraints)	
8. Refer when appropriate to employee assistance programs, career counselors, or other specialists for the administration, scoring, and interpreting of assessments	
9. Identify the coachee's learning style	

4. DEVELOPMENT PLANNING

To what degree is this person currently capable of doing the following as an executive coach?

Rating Scale
4 = Very capable
3 = Moderately capable

2 = Somewhat capable
1 = Hardly capable or not capable at all

	DEVELOPMENT PLANNING TASK/SKILL AREA	RATING
1.	Partner with Human Resources	
2.	Conduct debriefing and feedback sessions with the coachee regarding the assessments and 360-degree results	
3.	Establish specific coaching goals (behavioral, cognitive, skills, business, relationships, etc.)	
4.	Help the coachee design and create action plans and a coaching timetable	
5.	Help the coachee, his/her boss, and HR to review assessment results within agreed-on guidelines for confidentiality and translate those results into actionable coaching strategies	
6.	Establish qualitative and quantitative measures of results for the coaching goals	
7.	Determine what can be achieved in coaching and recommend appropriate training and other methods to achieve other developmental goals	
8.	Quickly identify the need for, and make referrals to, other helping professionals	
9.	Gain commitment for the coachee's self-management of coaching action plans	
10.	Help the boss to provide useful feedback and to coach the coachee as his/her manager	

5. FACILITATING DEVELOPMENT AND CHANGE

To what degree is this person currently capable of doing the following as an executive coach?

Rating Scale
4 = Very capable
3 = Moderately capable
2 = Somewhat capable
1 = Hardly capable or not capable at all

FACILITATING DEVELOPMENT AND CHANGE TASK/SKILL AREA	RATING
1. Take the coachee's point of view and offer alternative points of view	
2. Show accurate empathy	
3. Listen actively and respectfully	
4. Communicate clearly, concisely, and directly	
5. Provide constructive feedback	
6. Observe the coachee's behavior in coaching sessions and provide real-time feedback	
7. Offer specific strategies and suggested behavior changes	
8. Demonstrate and serve as a role model in the coaching for new work methods and ways of communicating	
9. Create and raise awareness	
10. Design assignments that encourage experimentation, reflection, and learning	

11. Ask powerful questions	
12. Support and confront appropriately	
13. Challenge assumptions	
14. Solicit solutions	
15. Swiftly translate ideas into action plans	
16. Develop management, executive, and leadership skills	
17. Provide learning resources as needed (reading, models, etc.)	
18. Involve the boss as the ongoing coach	
19. Measure and monitor the coaching process and results	
20. Address new issues and learning opportunities as they arise	
21. Be aware of and recognize your own part as the coach in the coachee's problem or situation through various methods (e.g., peer supervision, consultation)	
22. Coach the boss to better support the coachee and his/her business and coaching objectives	

6. ENDING FORMAL COACHING AND TRANSITIONING TO LONG-TERM DEVELOPMENT

To what degree is this person currently capable of doing the following as an executive coach?

Rating Scale

4 = Very capable

3 = Moderately capable

2 = Somewhat capable

1 = Hardly capable or not capable at all

ENDING FORMAL COACHING AND TRANSITIONING THE LONG-TERM DEVELOPMENT TASK/SKILL AREA	RATING
1. Identify the appropriate ending point in the formal coaching process	
2. Initiate discussion with the coachee, his/her manager, and others in the organization about bringing the formal coaching to an end	
3. Work with the coachee to identify ongoing developmental supports and resources in his/her environment and to establish a transition/ending plan	
4. Work with the coachee to establish postcoaching developmental goals and a plan for meeting those goals	
5. Work toward and encourage the coachee's independence	
6. Encourage the coachee to continue learning on his/her own	
7. Conduct formal ending meeting with the coachee, his/her manager, and Human Resources	
8. Leave the possibility open for future coaching as the need arises and within the guidelines of the coaching contract	

Comments on executive coaching tasks and skills:

_____

_____

_____

_____

GENERAL ATTRIBUTES AND ABILITIES

Categories
1. Mature self-confidence
2. Positive energy
3. Assertiveness
4. Interpersonal sensitivity
5. Openness and flexibility
6. Goal orientation
7. Partnering and influence
8. Continuous learning and development
9. Integrity

1. MATURE SELF-CONFIDENCE

To what degree does this person demonstrate the following attributes and abilities?

Rating Scale
4 = A great deal
3 = Quite a bit
2 = Somewhat
1 = Hardly or not at all

MATURE SELF-CONFIDENCE ATTRIBUTE OR ABILITY	RATING
1. Appears comfortable with him/herself	
2. Shows maturity; demonstrates that he/she has gained wisdom from personal and professional experience	

3. Shows confidence; places an appropriate value on his/her own abilities and perspectives	
4. Shows humility; demonstrates awareness that success usually follows from the efforts of a group or team of other individuals, not solely from one's own efforts	

2. POSITIVE ENERGY

To what degree does this person demonstrate the following attributes and abilities?

Rating Scale
4 = A great deal
3 = Quite a bit
2 = Somewhat
1 = Hardly or not at all

POSITIVE ENERGY ATTRIBUTE OR ABILITY	RATING
1. Shows energy, optimism, and enthusiasm	
2. Effectively manages his/her emotions	
3. Demonstrates resilience; bounces back after mistakes and failures	
4. Demonstrates an appropriate sense of humor	
5. Helps the coachee to appreciate his/her strengths and ability to overcome barriers	
6. Helps the coachee to imagine new possibilities	
7. Conveys hopefulness	

3. ASSERTIVENESS

To what degree does this person demonstrate the following attributes and abilities?

Rating Scale
4 = A great deal
3 = Quite a bit
2 = Somewhat
1 = Hardly or not at all

ASSERTIVENESS ATTRIBUTE OR ABILITY	RATING
1. Asserts him/herself and appropriately says "no" to set limits	
2. Confronts coachees and others who are not following through on commitments	
3. Speaks directly with others even when discussing difficult or sensitive issues	
4. Addresses conflict with others directly and constructively	
5. Communicates in ways that reflect respect for one's own worth and the worth of others	

4. INTERPERSONAL SENSITIVITY

To what degree does this person demonstrate the following attributes and abilities?

Rating Scale
4 = A great deal
3 = Quite a bit
2 = Somewhat
1 = Hardly or not at all

Interpersonal Sensitivity Attribute or Ability	Rating
1. Shows empathy with others	
2. Is sensitive to how his/her style impacts others or fits with the needs of others	
3. Demonstrates an interest in people; shows curiosity about the lives, goals, experiences, and perspectives of others	
4. Shows compassion and demonstrates concern for the needs and emotional well-being of others	
5. Demonstrates tact; gives difficult or critical information to others in a respectful and supportive fashion	
6. Learns and remembers other people's most important concerns	
7. Uses active listening techniques (e.g., maintaining full attention, periodically summarizing, being nonjudgmental) to reflect and acknowledge other people's feelings and concerns	

5. OPENNESS AND FLEXIBILITY

To what degree does this person demonstrate the following attributes and abilities?

Rating Scale
4 = A great deal
3 = Quite a bit
2 = Somewhat
1 = Hardly or not at all

	OPENNESS AND FLEXIBILITY ATTRIBUTE OR ABILITY	RATING
1.	Is able to understand and appreciate perspectives that differ from his/her own	
2.	Tailors his/her own approach to fit the preferences and needs of the coachee	
3.	Demonstrates flexibility; changes course or approach when the situation demands it	
4.	Understands and relates to individuals and groups from a variety of cultures with values different from his/her own culture	
5.	Seeks out and uses feedback to enhance the coaching engagement	

6. GOAL ORIENTATION

To what degree does this person demonstrate the following attributes and abilities?

Rating Scale
4 = A great deal
3 = Quite a bit
2 = Somewhat
1 = Hardly or not at all

	GOAL ORIENTATION ATTRIBUTE OR ABILITY	RATING
1.	Sets challenging but achievable goals for him/herself	
2.	Helps coachees to identify and set realistic and challenging goals	
3.	Is highly motivated toward the pursuit of his/her goals	

4. Shows resourcefulness; seeks out, or helps others seek out solutions under difficult or challenging conditions	
5. Demonstrates stability; stays on tasks for extended periods of time	
6. Shows persistence; does not give up when faced with a challenge	
7. Demonstrates the ability to organize work; effectively plans and manages resources and time when pursuing a goal	

7. PARTNERING AND INFLUENCE

To what degree does this person demonstrate the following attributes and abilities?

Rating Scale
4 = A great deal
3 = Quite a bit
2 = Somewhat
1 = Hardly or not at all

PARTNERING AND INFLUENCE ATTRIBUTE OR ABILITY	RATING
1. Carefully plans and tailors his/her own words in ways that achieve the desired impact	
2. Presents arguments that address others' most important concerns and issues	
3. Involves others as partners in a process to gain their support and buy-in	

4. Shows interest in and comfort with the context in which the coaching is taking place (for-profits, not-for-profits, health-care organizations, the public sector, marketing, finance, sales, R&D, etc.)	
5. Shares some of the values of people in the organization in which the coaching is taking place; has a fundamental comfort with private enterprise and/or public endeavors	
6. Demonstrates inclusiveness by encouraging the participation of multiple stakeholders	

8. CONTINUOUS LEARNING AND DEVELOPMENT

To what degree does this person demonstrate the following attributes and abilities?

Rating Scale
4 = A great deal
3 = Quite a bit
2 = Somewhat
1 = Hardly or not at all

CONTINUOUS LEARNING AND DEVELOPMENT ATTRIBUTE OR ABILITY	RATING
1. Seeks feedback to enhance overall coaching effectiveness	
2. Assesses and addresses gaps in his/her own knowledge and skill	
3. Undertakes study and learning to enhance skills that will contribute to the coaching he/she provide	

9. INTEGRITY

To what degree does this person demonstrate the following attributes and abilities?

Rating Scale
4 = A great deal
3 = Quite a bit
2 = Somewhat
1 = Hardly or not at all

INTEGRITY ATTRIBUTE/ABILITY	RATING
1. Takes and holds an ethical stand regardless of financial or other pressures	
2. Carefully maintains appropriate confidentiality in all dealings	
3. Determines what is appropriate through careful contracting in his/her coaching and consulting relationships, with the goal of meeting the needs of all stakeholders	
4. Demonstrates personal integrity; "walks the talk"	
5. Appears genuine, honest, and straightforward regarding his/her agenda and needs	
6. Focuses on and puts the client's needs ahead of his/her own	
7. Makes and keeps commitments to others	
8. Avoids a coaching workload that compromises the quality of the coaching service	
9. Respects the established relationships between the client and other providers of coaching, consulting, and/or other services	

Comments on general attributes and abilities:

_____

_____

_____

_____

Other comments:

_____

_____

_____

_____

PROFESSIONAL DEVELOPMENT PLAN

Review the results of your self-assessment and any 360-degree feedback you have received. Then complete this worksheet to summarize the components of your Professional Development Plan.

1. Greatest Strengths to Leverage

GREATEST STRENGTHS	WAYS TO LEVERAGE THESE STRENGTHS	COMMENTS/NOTES
Coaching knowledge		
Psychological knowledge		
Business acumen		
Organizational knowledge		
Executive coaching tasks and skills		
General attributes and abilities		

2. Greatest Opportunities for Professional Development as an Executive Coach

GREATEST OPPORTUNITIES FOR PROFESSIONAL DEVELOPMENT	WAYS TO DEVELOP IN THESE AREAS	COMMENTS/NOTES
Coaching knowledge		
Psychological knowledge		
Business acumen		
Organizational knowledge		
Executive coaching tasks and skills		
General attributes and abilities		

3. Attributes or Gaps in Ability for Which to Compensate

ATTRIBUTES OR GAPS IN ABILITY THAT REQUIRE COMPENSATION	WAYS TO COMPENSATE	COMMENTS/NOTES
Attributes		
Gaps in ability		

EXECUTIVE COACHING PROFESSIONAL DEVELOPMENT STRATEGIES

Strategies to Leverage Your Strengths

Use your greatest strengths to increase your effectiveness and build your value as an executive coach. Here are some examples of strategies that will capitalize on your strengths:

- Publish
- Conduct research
- Highlight your strengths in your promotional material
- Do public speaking
- Teach others
- Consult or subcontract to other coaches
- Develop a special consulting or coaching service
- Develop tools and special materials to use in your practice
- Post information and guides on your web site
- Develop a Web-based or hard-copy newsletter
- Form a professional association or group
- Lead a conference
- Sell targeted products or services
- Select an area in which to become a recognized expert; use your existing strengths to build and market that expertise

Strategies to Develop Knowledge and Skills
- Enroll in academic courses
- Read
- Take continuing education workshops
- Work with a mentor
- Hire your own coach
- Work in collaboration with other coaches who are strong in the area in which you need development
- Do research
- Take on a stretch assignment
- Work as an apprentice with an expert
- Complete a certification or degree
- Practice using a standard protocol
- Observe yourself on videotape
- Get feedback from clients
- Get feedback from experts
- Log or record journal entries to track your experiences and progress
- Establish specific, time-driven, measurable development goals
- Teach others

- Attend conferences
- Join a peer-supervision group
- Hire a supervisor
- Get a position in a consulting firm where you can be supervised and learn from other experts
- Volunteer or provide reduced-fee services that give you the opportunity to build your skills

Strategies to Compensate for Gaps in Attributes or Abilities
- Use structured systems
- Build a toolbox to guide your coaching activities
- Meet regularly with a coach, counselor, or supervisor to review your work and get objective feedback, guidance, and support
- Develop new approaches that force you to do what does not come naturally to you (e.g., active listening, assertiveness, relaxation, writing things down before responding, time management)
- Practice techniques until they become ingrained
- Get coaching or counseling for "cognitive restructuring" to challenge your irrational or nonconstructive beliefs or assumptions
- Learn new models of thinking to rely on when you are inclined to do something less constructive
- Join a support group to share guidance, encouragement, and reinforcement for what you find difficult or uncomfortable but need to do
- Choose coaching assignments that rely on your strengths rather than weaker areas where you are less able or have difficulty learning
- Accept who you are and present yourself with what you do best instead of what you wish you did better
- Rely on your secondary strengths
- Be careful not to overuse or misuse your natural strengths
- Reassess your old assumptions about yourself and your limitations as a reality check on what you can do
- "Walk before you run" when you try new approaches or skills.

- Give yourself time to learn and change
- Hire people to assist you in areas where you are less able or comfortable and don't want to learn or adapt (accounting, technology, marketing, writing, etc.)

Your Executive Coaching Professional Development Time Line

DEVELOPMENTAL OPPORTUNITIES	WHAT TO DO THIS YEAR	WHAT TO DO NEXT YEAR	WHAT TO DO THE YEAR AFTER NEXT
Greatest strengths to leverage			
1. 2. 3.			
Greatest opportunities for development			
1. 2. 3.			
Greatest needs that require compensation			
1. 2. 3.			

CHAPTER THREE

Building and Marketing Your Value Proposition as an Executive Coach

Many people who consider going into the professional practice of executive coaching can't imagine themselves as salespeople, going door to door to present themselves as the best coach in the world. Happily for us, executive coaches don't sell in traditional ways like car or insurance salespeople. This chapter is built on the assumptions of a consultative selling model.

What Is a Value Proposition?

With consultative selling, you aren't trying to convince a potential client to hire you as a coach. Instead, you are attracting the kind of client who would want to consider you. You sell your services by showing what you can do and how you do it rather than convincing prospects you have what they want. In this process of "showing," you learn about your potential clients and their unmet needs; and they have an opportunity to see you work and begin to trust you. For this model to succeed, the potential clients you attract must appreciate what you have to offer and want to "buy" your coaching when they see it in action. You need to build your true *value proposition* and market it to those people and organizations who will value you and your coaching services.

An executive coach's value proposition is the reason why potential clients choose one coach over another. As you build yourself as a professional executive coach, you are already developing several components of your value proposition. You base your coaching on a foundation of strong theory and evidence and conduct your practice according to professional standards. You are well trained, ethical, take a collaborative approach, and focus on helping coachees be better leaders and achieve results for their organization. But many other executive coaches offer the same value. To differentiate yourself, you must define for your prospective clients what is special about you and influence your target markets to perceive you in that light. To compete successfully, you continually redefine your practice to keep up with the ever-changing market.

Many unsuccessful executive coaches try to build their value propositions by first asking what the market, or clients in general, want. Although a value proposition does need to target the unmet needs of a market, don't try to build your practice on too general a marketplace. It may be a cliché, but you must first be true to yourself as a professional executive coach. Coming up with a value proposition that attracts many potential clients may be the easy part. More difficult is creating a value proposition that accurately reflects what you want to do, what meets your needs, what you are best at, and how potential clients will see you. If you don't, you'll fall into a common trap of generating lots of leads that don't develop into actual jobs, failing in the coaching you do conduct, and remaining unsatisfied in or unable to sustain your practice.

To increase the likelihood that you will attract the right potential clients, be selected as their coach, succeed at the coaching, and obtain satisfaction from your practice, there are four basic questions to answer before building your true value proposition:

1. What are your goals for conducting your professional executive coaching practice?

2. What is the special value you bring to your potential clients?
3. What executive coaching services will you offer?
4. Which market segments and clients would be attracted to your services and to you as a coach?

These four questions are relevant regardless of the form your coaching practice takes: internal coach in an organization, independent practitioner, member of a consulting firm, part of a network of coaches, or any other type of coaching situation. In this chapter, you'll answer these questions, build a value proposition based on your answers, and develop a plan to market and build your practice. That plan will be based on a value proposition that is true to you and your goals while fitting your chosen markets.

What Are Your Goals for Conducting Your Professional Executive Coaching Practice?

There are three types of goals: personal, career, and business. When you conduct any professional practice, and especially executive coaching, it is important to consider not only your business goals and requirements such as revenue, benefits, and building up assets, but also what you hope to accomplish at this point along your career path and this time in your life.

PERSONAL GOALS There are many avenues to achieving your personal goals: family and friends; community, religious, or professional affiliations; political or volunteer work; spiritual connections, and serving the environment. Professional work is another avenue. Some of my executive coaching students go into the field to make a difference in people's lives; others to learn, influence world leadership, have a flexible work schedule, travel, or help people in a practical, action-oriented way. Most of us have lifelong ambitions that go beyond simple career and financial goals to who we are and what we hope to accomplish with our lives.

The following questions will help you identify your personal goals for conducting a coaching practice, both in general and at this specific time in your life. As you answer each question, consider how you will conduct your practice to help you achieve these goals:

- What do you value most in life: money, recognition, productivity, social contact, being in a certain environment, and so on?
- What do you need to be comfortable and happy?
- What nurtures and feeds you?
- What do you want to give up or stop doing? Do you want to head in a different direction?
- What contributions do you want to make to the world?
- What do you wish you had accomplished in your life so far?
- What have you done that has given you the greatest satisfaction?
- Whom do you admire the most?
- What are the gaps between the ideal you and who you are today?
- What feedback regarding who you are as a person have you received from people you respect and care about?
- What personal challenges do you face? Are there any conditions or limitations that you need to overcome or compensate for? Physical, intellectual, stylistic, psychological, social?
- What are your natural abilities and special talents that you would like to apply to make the most of yourself?
- What do the people you want to please tell you to change about how you live your life and interact with them?
- In the world at large, and in the smaller world in which you live, what bothers you most? Do you wish you could change it?
- What causes do you want to support: social, political, spiritual, environmental, economic, and so on?
- What unfulfilled personal goals have you had for many years?
- How would you like to be seen by others?
- What would make you proud?
- What do others do that causes you to respect them?
- What would you like to be remembered for?

CAREER GOALS   People often evolve into a career without purpose and intention. But even when the route to a career is serendipitous, once there, it is satisfying to work in more than just a random assortment of jobs. As a professional, you often associate with others who do similar work. You have a stronger identity with your career than with a short-term job. People who go into executive coaching usually have both short- and long-term goals for moving forward along a career path—they want to work for more than money or to be productive. Use your preferences and objectives to guide your plan for building and managing your professional practice.

Use the following questions to help identify your career goals as a professional executive coach:

- What interests you most? What fascinates or intrigues you?
- What kinds of work activities do you most enjoy?
- What are your greatest abilities, strengths, and talents that you would like to apply at work?
- For which work activities do you get the most positive feedback from others?
- What potential areas of competence would you like to develop?
- What types of people or their attributes do you deal with best?
- What do you imagine and dream about doing professionally?
- How do you measure your success at work? What measures are the most meaningful to you?
- With which peers do you get the most satisfaction working?
- What are your long-term career objectives? What do you want to accomplish? What do you want to become professionally?
- How do you want to conduct yourself professionally as you strive to achieve your long-term career objectives (ethics, standards, relationships, etc.)?
- What are your short-term career objectives? What do you want to accomplish, keep the same, or change in the next two to three years?
- What work environments and cultures do you want to work in or avoid?

- How independently do you want to work? Do you want to control what you do and how you do it, or follow the direction and standards of others?

BUSINESS GOALS   Many people enter into or expand their work in executive coaching for business reasons as well as personal and career goals. You may, for example, have certain revenue objectives, an acceptable level of legal risk, or a business structure or entity through which you want to practice your coaching. Many of the people who study with me and ask for help developing their coaching practices do little thinking about business goals. They don't develop a realistic business scenario that could rule in or out the possibility of becoming an executive coach. Nor do they make business decisions in advance that allow them to achieve their minimum business requirements. As you consider your executive coaching plans, use the following questions to identify your business goals and requirements. Then test those requirements against realistic business projections:

- What is your long-term vision for your coaching practice? What will it look like in three to five years?
- What is the mission of your practice? What do you want to do? For whom? For what purpose?
- What are your overall strategic goals three to five years out?
- What approaches will you use to achieve those goals?
- How will you apply those approaches?
- What levels of leadership do you want to coach: board leaders, chief executives, middle managers, supervisors, professionals, others?
- What industries do you want, and don't want, to work in?
- What other products or consulting services will you provide apart from or together with your coaching services?
- How will you generate leads?
- How much profit do you want to clear on an annual basis—in the next year, two years, three years, and the longer term?

- What other financial goals and requirements do you have for your practice? For example, do you want to build up assets to sell or pass on, minimize taxes, reduce overhead costs, reduce your reliance on other sources of income, generate revenue by managing other coaches?
- How much are you able and willing to invest in building your practice in the next one, two, and three years? Consider infrastructure, materials, marketing and publicity, travel, professional support services (legal, accounting, insurance), time, and other resources.
- What are your requirements and preferences about the form of your practice? Do you want to work as an employee coaching leaders and potential leaders in your organization? As an employee of a consulting or coaching firm? As an associate or adjunct coach who takes on coaching projects of that firm's clients? As an independent coach? As part of a formal or informal network or partnership of coaches?
- If you want to work independently or in partnership with other coaches, in what form of legal entity do you want to practice — sole proprietorship, partnership, professional corporation, C-corporation, S-corporation, limited liability company, and nonprofit entity? (See www.sba.gov for pros and cons of various business entities.)
- What support staff will you employ to handle office management, administration, bookkeeping, telecommunications, technology, and so on?
- Do you want to limit your practice? Will you contract only with organizations to coach their employees, or with individuals too? Will you restrict the individuals or organizations for which you work (socially responsible organizations, geographic limitations, certain types of coaching or coaching assignments, and the like)?
- How will you limit or specialize your practice to work, or not work, with any organizational functions or departments?

- Do you want to limit the vehicles through which you will conduct coaching—face-to-face, phone, videoconferencing, and e-mail or electronic dialogues?
- If you do face-to-face coaching, will you limit where you will meet with your clients (at their offices, at your offices, off-site)?
- How much of your time do you want to spend working (hours or days per week or month, months per year)?
- How much work time will you commit to providing services at no or reduced cost, as a professional contribution or to give back to the community?
- How will you charge your clients—by the project, time spent, results, retainer?

 What Special Value Do You Bring to Your Potential Clients?

Clients seek you out as an executive coach based on the value they perceive you to bring, the potential benefit of your coaching, their comfort level with you and your approach, and overall cost. Because you are probably not the only available executive coach, you must differentiate yourself. Besides demonstrating that your service is worth the time and cost, you must show clients that you are the coach who best matches their needs and preferences.

In Chapter 2, you identified your strengths and weaknesses in executive coaching knowledge, skills, abilities, and attributes. Using those findings, what you know about yourself in other areas of your life, and what others tell you, define the value you bring to your target markets. Value falls into the following six categories:

1. Your special knowledge,
2. Your special skills,
3. Your special abilities,
4. Your special attributes,
5. Your special experience, and
6. Other competencies, characteristics, background, the services you offer, or the ways you manage your practice that clients may perceive as providing special value.

What Executive Coaching Services Will You Offer?

As described in Chapter 1, executive coaching is a complex and multifaceted field. People who call themselves executive coaches range from presentation-skills coaches to 360-degree survey-feedback experts, career counselors, leadership-development trainers, team-building consultants, and merger-and-acquisition advisors, to mention just a few. By the definition provided in Chapter 1, any and all of these types of activities may be components of an executive coaching practice. To represent yourself as a professional executive coach, you must define the scope and form of your practice.

As a collaborative, systems-oriented, leadership-development and results-focused coach, you can vary your practice greatly. The checklist in Table 3.1 lists many of the services offered by executive coaches. Use it to help you define the scope of your practice. Select those areas that best fit with the special value you bring to the market and the goals of your practice.

Which Market Segments and Clients Would Be Attracted to Your Services and to You as a Coach?

It's a lot easier to develop interest in your services and promote yourself by targeting your market and selling to organizations that are best matched to you and your practice. Based on the goals for your coaching practice, your value proposition, the coaching services you want to provide, and what you care about most when it comes to the organizations, which of the following markets and market segments are the right ones for your practice? (These lists are by no means exhaustive.)

Industries and Industry Segments
- Financial services
- Engineering and construction
- Education
- Health services and products

Table 3.1 Defining the Scope of Your Executive Coaching Practice

EXECUTIVE COACHING SERVICES	PLACE A CHECK MARK NEXT TO THE SERVICES YOU PLAN TO PROVIDE
360-degree interviews/surveys	
Assessments	
Feedback and development planning	
Team coaching	
High-potential coaching	
On-boarding coaching	
Remedial coaching	
Group coaching	
Legacy coaching	
Targeted coaching	
Coaching focused on interpersonal communication	
Coaching focused on strategic leadership	
Developmental coaching (focused on building self-awareness and removing internal individual barriers to success)	
Coaching focused on career development and career-life balance	
Coaching focused on building management skills and practices	

Table 3.1 *(Continued)*

Executive Coaching Services	Place a Check Mark Next to the Services You Plan to Provide
Coaching focused on achieving short-term, project-oriented results	
Specialized coaching in conjunction with organizational consulting	
Coaching internal and/or external coaches and human resource professionals on their coaching of others	
Other coaching services:	

- Government and the public sector
- Information services
- Manufacturing
- Professional and business services
- Natural resources
- Hospitality and leisure
- Retail and wholesale
- Engineering and construction
- Transportation and delivery
- Power and utilities
- Real estate
- Media
- Aerospace
- Marketing and advertising
- Venture capitalism

Organizational Culture and Values
- Human resources management
- Customer and client services

- Quality standards
- Management style
- Team orientation
- Organizational hierarchy and formality
- Policies and procedures
- Communication
- Decision making
- Loyalty
- Priorities
- Workload
- Openness
- Diversity
- Conflict management
- Pace
- Sources of power
- Consistency with stated philosophy
- Social responsibility
- Mission
- Stated and unstated values
- Innovation
- Risk
- Approaches to dealing with consultants and coaches

Organizational Entities
- Corporations
- Partnerships
- Family businesses
- Small businesses
- Professional service firms
- Nonprofits
- Government agencies
- Educational institutions

Geographic Locations
- National
- International

- Within a certain distance or travel time from your home or main office
- Limitations or preferences for working with certain geographic regions or countries

Organizational Functions
- General management
- Finance and accounting
- Operations
- Marketing
- Sales
- Legal and regulatory
- Research and development
- Service delivery
- Quality
- Communications and public relations
- Investor relations
- Information technology
- Administration
- Human resources
- Labor relations
- Risk management
- Facilities, security, and real estate development
- Transportation
- Strategic planning
- Training and development
- Distribution
- Governance and board relations
- Industry-specific functions (hospital emergency department or nursing, higher-education alumni relations, government public safety, nonprofit fund-raising, etc.)

Coachee Roles and Levels
- Board officers
- Chief executives
- General managers

- Department heads
- Human resources executives
- Middle managers
- Project managers
- Technical leaders

Other Market Characteristics and Situations
- Start-ups
- Highly competitive markets
- Mergers and acquisitions
- Organizations in crisis
- Financial recovery situations
- Downsizing situations
- Major organizational change

YOUR PROFESSIONAL EXECUTIVE COACHING VALUE PROPOSITION

You have asked yourself and hopefully answered the questions about your personal goals, the special value you will offer your clients, services to provide, and market segments on which to focus. Your answers to these four basic questions are the building blocks for your true value proposition as a professional executive coach. Now you must assemble these blocks into a proposition that will appeal to your target markets.

Your proposition may take many forms as described next. You can use all of these marketing forms and materials to bring your value proposition to life and attract potential clients. Your goal in formulating a value proposition is to communicate to prospective clients that you can best meet their needs, not to entice them to select you even if another coach would serve them better. In fact, you have an obligation to refer a potential client to other coaches or consultants when you know it would be to the client's benefit. By sharing your value proposition with other professionals, you will be in a position to refer prospects and receive referrals yourself.

Answer these questions to build your professional executive coaching value proposition:

1. What do you help leaders do?

   _____

   _____

2. How do you help them do it?

   _____

   _____

3. What knowledge, abilities, and skills make you especially capable of coaching leaders and would-be leaders?

   _____

   _____

4. What experience do you bring to help your clients?

   _____

   _____

5. What about you, who you are, how you think, your style, and how you work differentiates you as a professional executive coach?

   _____

   _____

6. What coaching services do you provide?

   _____

   _____

7. What types of people do you work best with? What about you and the way you work makes you the best coach for those clients?

   _____

   _____

8. What is your passion for coaching? Why do you coach, and what impact do you hope to achieve?

   _____

   _____

DEVELOPING A PLAN TO BUILD AND MARKET YOUR PRACTICE

The consultative sales approach to building your practice sets you up for success by targeting and attracting a market well matched to you and what you have to offer. Once you identify your target market, your next step is to make yourself known to people and organizations in that market. You also want to build a partnership with those organizations so they will include you in their planning for future leadership development. Because so many coaching opportunities come through referrals, you also need to develop a reliable and diversified referral network. Additional sources for leads include other types of leadership development experts and organizational consultants, plus people with contacts in your target market. Finally, once a referral source or potential client contacts you, respond in a way that maximizes your chances of matching the right clients.

The following sections provide guidance on:

- Building awareness of you and your services in your target market,
- Establishing and managing partnerships with organizations in those markets,
- Developing and maintaining a reliable and diversified referral network, and
- Preparing yourself to respond positively to referrals or requests to explore potential coaching situations.

Building Market Awareness

The first step is to research your target markets. The answers to the follow questions will help you build market awareness of you and your services:

- What are the current and future coaching needs in target market organizations?

98

- Who needs coaching (level, positions, organizations, etc.)?
- What are the current unmet needs of organizations?
- What are their future coaching needs?
- How do organizations find and select executive coaches?
- What do they care about most when selecting coaches?
- What fees are they used to paying for coaching services?
- What do potential coachees read?
- What meetings do they attend?
- With whom do they associate?
- What are the target organizations' past, present, and future patterns of using executive coaching?
- Where do they obtain referrals?
- Who makes the ultimate buying decisions for coaching?
- What is their business environment, and what will it be in the months and years ahead?

This information is not only relevant concerning potential coachees. It is also valuable data to collect on the bosses of the leaders to be coached, the organization's human resource professionals and business consultants, and other groups and people who provide coaching services. You can conduct this research through a variety of means, including:

- Reading books, articles, annual reports, investment analyses, and industry journals
- Talking with experts in the field and region
- Conducting exploratory consultative meetings with representatives in prospective client organizations
- Going to association meetings, conferences, and events attended by referral sources, potential coachees, and people who make coaching decisions for their organizations
- Conducting formal market research or hiring marketing experts to do the research (interviews, surveys, focus groups, etc.)

ELEVATOR SPEECHES In today's fast-paced world, you often have a minute or less to introduce yourself and your coaching services—the length of an elevator ride. The goal of an elevator speech is not, obviously, to tell all. It's to say enough for the other person to follow up or remember you when someone is looking for a coach.

Your elevator speech should be tailored to the market and individual based on the research you have done about their situation, needs, and preferences. It isn't a sales pitch as much as an overview of who you are, what you do, and how you do it as a coach. An easy way to build your elevator speech is to review your answers to the value proposition questions earlier in this chapter, jotting down a few phrases that summarize who you are as a coach and what you have to offer.

Let's assume that an executive coach is meeting with a leader to explore the possibility of providing coaching. While at the prospect's company, the coach runs into a human resources manager who says, "I heard you were going to be here to talk about doing some coaching. Do you do a lot of executive coaching?" Here is the coach's elevator speech:

> I do a lot of consulting and coaching in your organization and in many others in the area. Most of my work is with middle- to upper-level managers individually as well as with teams. All of my coaching is customized, and my 20 years of experience in organizational and executive development allow me to deal with a wide variety of coaching situations. I specialize in preparing high potential people for leadership assignments. Would you like to get together sometime for lunch to talk about your coaching needs and how I might help?

BROCHURES, WEB SITES, AND OTHER MATERIALS   Brochures, web sites, and other descriptions of you and your services allow you to build market awareness and provide information about your services when someone expresses interest. The art and science of marketing materials is complex. The following ten guidelines will help you develop brochures, advertising copy, collateral material, newsletters, and web sites that will influence potential clients to contact you.

Ten Guidelines for Building Marketing Materials

1. Focus your marketing materials on specific target markets. The more you try to make your message appropriate for a wide audience, the less it will resonate with specific individuals.

2. Don't rely on one medium or marketing activity and wait for a response that rarely comes. Successful marketing uses multiple media with repeated communications to get a memorable message out.

3. Build your marketing materials for your clients, not for you. Executive coaches often spend time and money coming up with a name or logo based on what they like instead of what would be attractive and appropriate for their target markets.

4. Avoid glitz, self-aggrandizement, and the hard sell—the feel of your materials should be professional. Colors, fonts, formats, and the overall first impression shouldn't make the potential client or referral source think of you as a TV commercial announcer. Keep the quality high and understated.

5. Keep it simple! Provide only enough information to entice your audience to talk with you. Make it easy for people to follow up with phone numbers, e-mail addresses, and web site or blog links. For web sites, use hyperlinks on short bullet points so the visitor can click for more details or e-mail you.

6. Use each piece of marketing material for one purpose. Don't go for one complex brochure that needs its own set of instructions to figure out.

7. Design your materials, or have them designed, for an audience with multiple perceptual preferences—visual, auditory, and so on. The written word is important but often less memorable than a picture, symbol, or sound.

8. Start small, and experiment with different kinds of materials and messages to see which ones generate the most interest and desired response. Build your marketing material based on experience with your target markets.

9. Focus on your homepage for your web site. It should be easy for people to find. Make the center of focus obvious and use tabs to provide information for different types of visitors.

10. Don't overuse marketing material instead of getting out there to network and build relationships with potential clients and referral sources. You are the best marketing materials for your practice.

TARGETED E-MAIL BLASTS   E-mail blasts are electronic mass mailings targeted to specific individuals by group. There are several ways to conduct e-mail blasts. The least expensive, but often most time consuming, is to build your own database and send group e-mails yourself. Software simplifies the process of e-mailing material to select groups within a database. A professional mass marketer can send out e-mails using either the addresses you provide or ones the marketer builds and maintains. Another option is to buy or lease e-mail address lists from marketing firms or associations and either send the blasts yourself or have the firm blast its list of contacts.

There are a variety of barriers to successful e-mail blasts. One of the most common is a spam blocker that prevents people from receiving your e-mail. This is especially true in large organizations with strong firewalls. Another common barrier is e-mail overload: your recipients may simply delete your e-mail without reading it. Rather than e-mailing the masses, do much more targeted mailings and follow up with phone calls or personalized letters. This strategy has much more impact than e-mail alone. A third common mistake is the failure to update e-mail lists. Because people often change employment or e-mail addresses, it is typical for a large number of e-mails to be returned as nondeliverable.

Over time you can build your own targeted e-mail databases and update them yourself, or employ an administrative assistant to manage your contact database. If you buy or lease an e-mail list, research how up-to-date it is before making the investment.

TARGETED MAILINGS   Like e-mail, the amount of hard-copy mail people in your target market receive is overwhelming. Why should they even open your letter? If they do read it, why should they remember it or contact you as a result? In most cases, they would not. But some potential buyers of coaching services are primarily influenced through hard-copy mail, and there are a few things you can do to increase the likelihood that your mailing will get through:

- Make your envelope or package positive, personalized, and attractive to prevent recipients from throwing it out without opening it.
- Getting recipients to open your mailing is just the first step, however. Inside, a simple message with a take-away that addresses a current need or interest should capture your readers' attention and entice them to read further.
- If you succeed in capturing their interest, make it simple for recipients to take action.

It is rare for these three factors to come together with a mass mailing. The more targeted the mailing, focused on a few key individuals with whom you can follow up within a short time, the more it will generate interest in you as a coach. Remember, you should not expect any one medium or message to generate a sale. But in conjunction with other marketing media, targeted mailings help to build awareness and interest in you and your services.

CONFERENCES AND ASSOCIATION MEETINGS   If you are comfortable and articulate talking with people at conferences or association meetings, attending them gives you an opportunity to build market awareness. Networking at conferences is also a good way to establish relationships with people who may have future coaching needs. Management associations, chambers of commerce, industry sectors, human resources associations, and specialty interest groups often hold meetings and conferences on leadership development or coaching. Rather than investing your time in one specific type of meeting or group, make the rounds and see which organizations will provide the best contacts with decision makers or referral sources in your target markets.

PRESENTATIONS TO LEADERSHIP TEAMS, CONFERENCES, AND OTHER GROUPS   One of the best ways to build market awareness is through formal presentations. At low or no cost, develop a presentation and use your network to get on the speaking docket. The best subjects to speak on are the ones that give you credibility as an expert in an area related to leadership, leadership development, or the leader's impact on organizational results. Topics include emotional intelligence, influence, leadership teams, strategic leadership, managing through turbulent times, doing more with less, customer focus, and the human side of mergers and acquisitions. Over time, assuming you are an effective presenter and come across as an expert, people will remember you and associate you with executive coaching. They may talk to other people about you. Developing and delivering an effective formal presentation will give you an effective tool for building market awareness and interest in your coaching services.

NEWSLETTERS   Many consultants send weekly, monthly, or quarterly newsletters to generate name recognition and provide clients, prospects, and referral sources with valuable information. The upside: after a period of time, the newsletter will make your name and approaches recognizable. But there is also a downside: few people have the time to read one more piece of mail (or e-mail), so your newsletter may backfire if your name becomes associated with junk mail. But it is worth trying a newsletter for a short period of time, perhaps six months to a year, to see if it generates a response. Just be sure *not* to make your newsletter a direct advertisement or sales pitch for your services. Instead, turn it into a valuable resource that addresses issues you have found to be important to your target market.

ARTICLES, BOOKS, AND OTHER PUBLICATIONS   Imagine that your target market and referral sources have been reading your e-mails and mailings, linking to your web site, talking with you at conferences, hearing you speak at meetings, and gathering valuable nuggets of information from your regular newsletter. They open up a journal, book, or newspaper, and there you are again—writing an article or chapter; hosting a regular column on leadership or coaching. This scenario takes time to create but builds your name recognition and respect as an expert in the field.

Dedicate several hours per week to writing pieces to submit for publication in the sources that your target market reads. And by networking with other authors who publish books, you may eventually get your own book contract and add another level of credibility to your market presence.

ADVERTISING   As a professional executive coach, traditional TV or radio ads may not be the best medium to create market demand for your services. But many other forms of advertising activities may help: sponsoring public radio or TV stations, financially supporting school or community events, cosponsoring conferences or special events, and participating in activities valued by your target market. If your market is localized, consider buying direct ads for your services in local papers or business publications. As with all marketing media, conduct research to determine the "reach" your advertisement will have into your target market. Needless to say, if you do any advertising, always present yourself in a professional way. Avoid any misleading claims, only represent yourself as an expert in areas where you have true expertise, respect the intellectual property of others, maintain client confidentiality, and avoid any conflicts of interest.

Building and Managing Partnerships

The emphasis in Chapter 1 was on the importance of building and managing partnerships with key people: potential coachees, their bosses, human resources professionals, and others involved with coaching in the organization. These partnerships are equally important as you build and market your value proposition. The differences between vendors and partners are significant and can have considerable impact on how you build your coaching practice.

Coaching vendors take orders, deliver the coaching services promised, and receive payment accordingly. They sell themselves to meet their sales forecasts. Coaching partners work more collaboratively with coachees and others in the client organization to identify and meet current and emerging coaching needs. Partners help potential clients figure out whether they require coaching and, if they do, find a coach who meets their needs.

Whether you are an internal coach or external consultant, working in partnership with potential clients builds your credibility. It also increases the chances that, when a suitable coaching situation arises, you will be part of the decision-making process. One of the best ways to build partnerships with potential clients is to invest in them. Consider the following activities:

- Devote the time to learn about their organization, business environment, competition, customers, and past, current, and projected business situation.
- Learn about their individual leaders.
- Meet with them and demonstrate your consulting and coaching skills without worrying about being paid at the beginning.
- Show your value proposition through your actions, which will speak louder any words.
- Go out of your way to help prospects figure out what they need and the best ways to satisfy those needs.
- Be proactive and responsive to build relationships.
- Continually reach out to check in without trying to sell yourself.

Once you have a coaching project, don't worry about counting minutes and giving away time. Take a broader, longer-term view of the client relationship. The more you give, usually the more you will receive in return.

Building and Maintaining a Reliable and Diversified Referral Network

As already discussed, a referral network is key to building a successful executive coaching practice. If you rely on only a few people for referrals, your opportunities are limited. The more widespread and diverse your referral sources, the more likely your name is to come up in situations appropriate for you. Here are some of the actions you should take:

- Build referral relationships by talking to people you know — and talk to their contacts, too.
- Seek and make connections with people in touch with your target markets.
- Schedule a certain amount of time each week for networking meetings.
- Make a predetermined number of phone calls per week to potential referral sources.
- When you make a good connection, share your value proposition with them. Ask them to share their value proposition with you.
- Be explicit with your referral sources. How will you refer clients to each other? Also be transparent with potential clients about your referral process.
- Meet with key referral sources to determine your level of comfort in referring business to one another. Exchange extra business cards and appropriate marketing materials to give potential clients upon making a referral.
- Stay in touch with clients you have referred to get feedback on their experience with that coach.

Because opportunities for coaching often arise during discussions of a noncoaching nature, don't limit your referral sources to other executive coaches. Remember that your goal is not only to get business for yourself, but also to help your referral sources get business. Most importantly, your role is to help people with leadership-development and business issues find the most appropriate resources to meet those needs. The following potential referral sources may all prove fruitful:

- Executive coaches with similar value propositions to yours
- Executive coaches with different value propositions
- Coaches who do other types of coaching

- Consultants who work with leaders and human resources professionals but do not do executive coaching
- Executive coaches from different geographic areas who are in contact with organizations in your region
- Internal human resources professionals who seek executive coaches for leaders in their organizations
- Friends and friends of friends who are in the position to talk with people in an organization who are looking for executive coaches

Preparing for and Responding to Referrals and Exploratory Discussions

The most important way to prepare for and respond to potential coaching situations is to think about those situations not as potential business leads, but rather as opportunities to help people find resources. Rather than selling yourself as a coach, increase your chances of being sought out and selected by helping people figure out what they need and the best ways to meet those needs. You will be showcasing your coaching skills and style as you do so.

For prospects to determine if you are a potential source of help, you need to be ready with your elevator speech and respond immediately when contacted by e-mail or phone. When you call or e-mail back, be prepared to refer prospects to your web site or send them collateral marketing material. Not only will they learn about you and your coaching practice, they'll also increase their knowledge about executive coaching in general and obtain guidelines for finding the right coach.

Schedule a face-to-face meeting if possible. Based on your preliminary phone and e-mail interactions, bring enough copies of relevant materials and referral information. After the meeting, immediately follow up with an e-mail, phone call, or thank you letter. Send additional materials based on what you learned at the meeting, and follow that up with a planned phone call if appropriate. It always pays off to invest in every lead, if not in financial terms then in terms of personal satisfaction—knowing you did the right thing by helping people get the help they need.

Assembling and Managing the Building Blocks of Your Executive Coaching Practice

The first three chapters of this book helped you answer five key questions about your professional executive coaching practice:

1. What is professional executive coaching?
2. Is it right for you?
3. How will you build your competencies in the field?
4. What is your unique value proposition?
5. How will you market your practice?

This chapter is about applying your answers to these questions so you will be ready to serve your clients. Whether you are an external consultant or internal coach, there are seven essential building blocks to building and managing your practice. After a brief introduction of these building blocks, the remainder of this chapter is devoted to discussing each one in detail.

ESSENTIAL BUILDING BLOCKS OF YOUR EXECUTIVE COACHING PRACTICE

Your Executive Coaching Network

Professional executive coaches acknowledge not only their areas of competence, but also the areas that others do better. In areas in which you are not sufficiently qualified, do not represent yourself as competent, permit others to represent you as such, or attempt to practice. To advise your clients best, you should continually seek multiple perspectives. For this you need the first essential building block: a network of professionals in executive coaching and other disciplines with whom you can consult and to whom you can refer clients and prospects. In some cases, it is appropriate to refer leaders to other professionals who have the expertise you may lack. Other times, even though you are the best overall resource, you may not be available or may need to consult others to tap their specialty knowledge and continue to build your own capabilities.

Your Executive Coaching Toolbox

Even if you were an expert at building houses, you couldn't build a house without the right tools. Executive coaching has its essential tools as well. Professional executive coaches base their work on strong, well-founded theories and models. They collaborate with the client's organization to plan and manage the coaching. They use evidence and data to focus their efforts, develop leaders, and achieve organizational results. And they work in a very practical way with their coachees. Your essential coaching toolbox is a wide and varied one.

Your Office Infrastructure

Whether it is an actual office space or a virtual one, it must be a hub of state-of-the-art, efficient, reliable, and responsive systems, processes, and technology that can meet the client's needs and expectations as well as your own. If you were a quality control expert, you would rely on hardware, software, databases, communication channels, statistical norms, and policies and procedures to provide cutting-edge services. So, too, does an executive coach need hardware, software, equipment, an extensive library, a financial management system, assessment devices, and a host of other infrastructure components. This infrastructure prevents you from reinventing the wheel every time your clients need something from you, you need something from them, or you are managing your practice.

Your Executive Coaching Management System

The fourth building block is your coaching project management process. Each coach has a methodology for managing coaching, and each coaching project should be customized to the needs of the individual and the organization. Building on the executive coaching principles and practices described in Chapter 1, the seven-step process illustrated in Figure 4.1 is one way to customize a project management system to fit your own approach and style as well as each individual coaching situation.

Professional and Peer Supervision

No matter how much experience you have, supervision enables you to continuously learn from peers and experts with more experience and objectivity than you may possess about a client situation. Professional and peer supervisors, mentors, and coaches provide confidential avenues for you to step back, reflect, and learn from your own experience and others' perspectives and best practices.

Research and Publication

Studying the research of others and conducting and reporting your own research takes time. But you must commit that time and build

Figure 4.1 Seven-Step Executive Coaching Management System

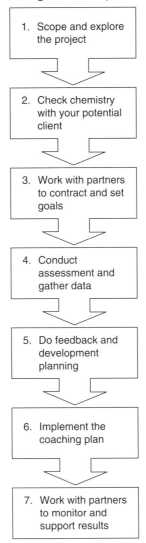

1. Scope and explore the project

2. Check chemistry with your potential client

3. Work with partners to contract and set goals

4. Conduct assessment and gather data

5. Do feedback and development planning

6. Implement the coaching plan

7. Work with partners to monitor and support results

it into your practice. Professional executive coaches learn from everything they do. We try out coaching strategies and approaches with varying results. We may be artists in our innovation, spontaneity, creativity, and expression; but we are also scientists in our systematic approaches, use of evidence and data, and observation of patterns and formulas about leadership, learning, and organizational effectiveness.

Our experience as coaches informs what leaders and other coaches do. You cannot, however, simply give advice and expect people to accept what you say without supplying data to back it up. Such data are often qualitative case descriptions and examples, but must also be quantitative. For our discipline to build and evolve, we cannot assume that what has worked in the past will work in the future. You must measure and monitor what you do, how you do it, and the results you obtain. Use not only stories, pictures, and theories to teach and advise, but also scientific data that you and others have collected. You should share these data in a public forum, in writing or through other media. Finally, your research and reporting must protect the confidentiality of your clients.

Community Service

As a professional executive coach, you can gain great personal benefit from community service, and you have a professional obligation to give back to the communities in which you practice. This service can come in many forms: pro bono coaching, speaking at professional conferences, writing articles or columns for local newspapers or business journals, or contributing time and talent to the world in which you live and work. Community service not only fulfills your responsibility as a professional executive coach — it is also one of the greatest sources of personal satisfaction.

How to Build and Manage Your Coaching Network

The composition of your coaching network will be determined by the focus and complexity of your practice. But the diversity and geographic range of the people you consult with and refer work to should not be limited by your professional background, theoretical or practical biases, or physical location. Coaches often fool themselves into believing that they know everything about their area of executive coaching. However, when they talk with other professionals from similar or different backgrounds, they discover how many other areas of knowledge and approaches there are to consider. Try as you might to remain open minded and eclectic about leadership, organization development, and practical approaches, it is all too easy to limit what and how you see without realizing it.

You may have received professional training as a psychologist, business manager, financial analyst, anthropologist, human resources specialist, systems analyst, or spiritual leader. Regardless of the discipline that you studied and with which you identify, you have a point of view and set of knowledge and skills that can be of great value as an executive coach. But be careful: Your area of specialization can also limit how you think about your clients' challenges and opportunities, what you read, what research you follow, and whom you talk with to gain insight and perspective. To avoid this trap, you owe it to your clients and yourself to reach across disciplines and seek out multiple paradigms, models, approaches, and networks of experts.

Don't limit yourself to reading professional journals from your formative discipline. Also attend conferences in areas about which you know little. Go out of your way to find experts who think differently about people, organizations, and businesses. Avoid defensiveness about your theoretical approach. Rather than focusing on what doesn't make sense to you about someone else's viewpoint, look for anything that triggers innovative strategies to help your clients.

Build your professional network with a multidisciplinary approach in mind. Start by considering the coaching services you offer. For each service, take into account all the situations or challenges you might face. Brainstorm alone and with others about disciplines and models useful to your practice, and contact experts in those disciplines. As an example, if you have extensive experience with one or two 360-degree feedback surveys, talk with people who use other instruments or have special expertise in conducting 360-degree qualitative interviews. If you are an expert on working with teams but have never worked with a team of lawyers, then consult with a coach who has that background. If you think you can't handle the project, refer it to a coach who can.

After reviewing the services you do offer, consider the ones you do not offer. Since it is unlikely that you will ever know enough to take on all coaching opportunities on your own, you need a network of experts to which you can refer clients. Either subcontract and maintain control over the project, or simply make a referral. Try to provide more than one alternative to the prospective client. Not only will you give the prospect a greater choice, but this will also limit your liability should anything go wrong with the work another consultant provides. Consider issues of control, liability, communication, planning, coordination, and ethics as you determine whether to subcontract or make a referral.

Do not coach people with whom you have a conflicting relationship or when the work represents a conflict of interest. Examples include family members, close friends, close colleagues, anyone whose financial or other interests are tied to yours, people who control your employment or destiny, or whose employment you control. Also avoid coaching leaders who work in organizations where you have a financial investment—your judgment may be affected by what benefits you personally.

It is very common for people you know in one part of your life to ask you to coach them or someone with whom they live, work, or associate. When a conflict of interest or dual relationship exists, it is not appropriate to serve as coach. The best way to deal with these situations is to make referrals to several other coaches. Maintain a network firewall to prevent inappropriate sharing of information, and restrain yourself from involvement.

Sometimes an organization needs coaching for two or more individuals in a boss-subordinate or other relationship, and it is inappropriate or less effective for one coach to work with everyone involved. It is not uncommon for a whole leadership team to be coached, including the team leader. In these situations, it is especially important to know other coaches with whom you work well since you may have to communicate and collaborate with them. Such contact should only take place if the client agrees and grants written permission. When you explore a potential relationship with a client, you may determine that additional resources would be beneficial in addition to coaching. If you have expertise in these other areas, provide your services only if your involvement does not represent a conflict of interest or dual relationship.

In many cases, the client may need to be referred to experts in areas other than coaching. Your network should include a variety of consultants who can provide those resources directly or help find them. Examples of noncoaching referral issues include legal, medical, spiritual, psychological, media and public relations, personal dress and appearance, training, security, organization development, human resources policies and administration, and financial management and investment.

The matrix in Table 4.1 will help you identify different kinds of referral and consulting resources for your network.

A referral and consulting network is by no means permanent. Once you build it, it needs constant tending. Coaches frequently change the services they provide, their professional affiliations, geographic and travel requirements, pricing, working arrangements, and contact information. Stay up-to-date on who is doing what, where, and how. Seek out new and different resources and update arrangements with others. Keep a written record on your changing network, and inform the members of your network as you and your practice evolve.

Use the following list to keep track of your referral and consulting network:

Professionals with areas of expertise stronger than yours:

_____

_____

Professionals who offer services you do not:

_____

_____

Table 4.1 Areas in Which to Build Your Referral and Consulting Network

COACHING SERVICES	BACKGROUNDS AND AREAS OF EXPERTISE OF YOUR REFERRAL AND CONSULTING NETWORK							
	PSYCHOLOGY	BUSINESS	COMMUNICATIONS	HUMAN RESOURCES	ORGANIZATIONAL DEVELOPMENT	RELIGION/ SPIRITUALITY	SCIENCE/ ENGINEERING	SOCIOLOGY
360-degree interviews/surveys								
Assessments								
Feedback and development planning								
Teams								
High-potentials								
On-boarding								
Remedial								
Group								

(continued)

Table 4.1 *(Continued)*

Coaching Services	Psychology	Business	Communications	Human Resources	Organizational Development	Religion/ Spirituality	Science/ Engineering	Sociology
Legacy								
Targeted								
Interpersonal communication								
Strategic leadership								
Developmental (building self-awareness and removing internal barriers to success)								
Career development and career-life balance								

Backgrounds and Areas of Expertise of Your Referral and Consulting Network

Building management skills and practices				
Achieving short-term, project-oriented results				
Specialized coaching in conjunction with organizational consulting				
Coaching internal and external coaches and HR professionals on their coaching of others				
Other coaching services				

Professionals with different theoretical approaches than yours:

_____

_____

Professionals from different disciplines:

_____

_____

Professionals who offer the same services as you do, to whom you can make referrals when you are not available, you need additional coaches to work with you or separately, or a conflict of interest or dual relationship exists:

_____

_____

Professionals who provide services other than executive coaching:

_____

_____

Other sources for referral or consulting:

_____

_____

A network is only as strong as its members' trust and motivation to collaborate. Maintain your relationships to make consulting and referrals work for you, the clients and prospects you are serving, and the members of your network. It takes a commitment of time, not only when you are looking for work but also when you are especially busy, but do not neglect it.

CREATING YOUR COACHING TOOLBOX

The word "tool" stems from the root meaning "instrument," "implement," and "preparation." Like the original "coach," the covered wagon that improved travel over rough terrain, your toolbox will make the work of coaching easier, faster, and often more comfortable for both you and your client.

We all have our jobs and hobbies that require tools. As an amateur woodworker, I buy tools off the shelf, order from special catalogs, or develop my own in response to a particular need. The simpler the tool and more generic its use, the easier it is to use off the shelf. The more complex and special the application, the more the tool needs to be retrofitted or developed from scratch. After many years, I have accumulated an assortment of woodworking tools and coaching tools, some of which I use constantly. Others are stored for the rare occasion they are required. Executive coaches often begin their practice with an assortment of off-the-shelf tools and others they have accumulated over the years of other work they have done. But it often takes many years of executive coaching to tailor and customize tools for special situations.

Executive coaching tools take many forms. For example, a theoretical model in words or graphic form can provide meaning and new ways of thinking about the leader's role, organization, or goals. There are models of motivation, influence, adult development, conflict, personality, economics, change, and systems. Some tools may be helpful in almost all executive coaching situations. Others are useful for specific, targeted coaching. Here is an overview of the tools you may need to have in your toolbox. They are listed by use and form. See the Appendix for references for these tools and other resources.

Essential Executive Coaching Toolbox

Tools Used in Most Executive Coaching Situations

- *Precoaching tools:* Examples—Coaching readiness assessment guide; agenda outline for initial meetings between coach, coachee, boss, and other members of the organization supporting the coaching.
- *Contracting tools:* Examples—Templates for formal coaching contracts; checklists of coaching options; sample ground rules for the coach and coachee to work together.
- *Assessment tools:* Examples—Standardized tests of personality, interest, ability, or style; observation guides; financial report cards; behavioral check sheets.

- *Goal-setting tools:* Examples — List of criteria for SMART goals; examples of coaching goals by type and level; template for planning coaching goals based on 360-degree feedback.
- *Tools for guiding and facilitating leadership development and the achievement of work:* Examples — Model of the stages of adult learning; measurement matrix of types of measures (results/ process, quantitative/qualitative); goal-achievement tracking software.
- *Tools to help transition from coaching to long-term development:* Examples — Template for long-term development plan; catalog of public leadership-development programs; coaching guidelines for the coachee's boss to reinforce and maintain the gains.

Tools for Achieving Specific Executive Coaching Goals

- *Career-life coaching tools:* Examples — Job selection criteria grid; values clarification worksheet; stress management techniques instructions.
- *Communication coaching tools:* Examples — Assertive statement template; presentation planning guide; videorecording equipment; body language interpretation guidelines; software for multimedia presentations.
- *Developmental coaching tools:* Examples — List of common irrational beliefs; exercise to write your own obituary if you had lived the ideal life; questionnaire to help identify developmental stage; case readings of people at different levels of self-actualization.
- *Leadership coaching tools:* Examples — Media presentation of inspirational leaders; strategic planning template; leadership; competencies profile; team-building exercises.
- *Management coaching tools:* Examples — Aids to performance checklist; delegation model and guidelines; time management and prioritization log; Web links to management associations, networks, and support material.

Sample Formats of Executive Coaching Tools

- Assessment instruments
- Card sorts

- Case studies
- Charts and diagrams
- Checklists and check sheets
- Decision-making criteria and matrices
- Demonstrations
- Examples of best practices
- Formulas
- Games
- Guided activities with instructions
- Links to other coaches and experts
- Logs to record activities and results
- Media presentations
- Networks and referral sources
- Normative databases and reference points
- Observation guides
- Practice exercises
- Rating scales
- Readings
- Software
- Surveys and questionnaires
- Techniques
- Technology and equipment
- Templates
- Web-based references and materials
- Written guidelines, instructions, and directions

BUILDING YOUR OFFICE INFRASTRUCTURE

If you are an individual coach working internally or externally and have a few coaching projects per year, you may need very little office infrastructure: a private workspace, a place to meet with people, a phone, a filing system, a computer linked to the Web, and a billing system. The more complex and extensive your coaching practice, the more infrastructure you need.

I have seen two common traps for coaches building a practice. The first is underestimating how much work you will get and the infrastructure you will need to support that work. The second is investing in an extensive infrastructure to support many clients before they materialize. From my experience, the best approach to building infrastructure is to let the demand for coaching services drive your investment rather than the other way around.

One of my colleagues invested hundreds of thousands of dollars on leasing a large office space; hiring other consultants and administrative staff; and buying technology, systems, and equipment. He did all this prior to contracting for any long-term projects to support his overhead costs. Within a short time, he had to let most of his staff go, sell his equipment, and pay off his lease. Another colleague who was an internal human resources professional gave up her work in employee relations and training to focus on providing executive coaching to senior leaders in her organization. She contracted with a consultant to do executive assessments, spent months developing a coaching process for the organization, and invested hundreds of thousands of dollars of the organization's time and money in preparation for offering coaching to the executive team. Within a year, it became evident that the senior leaders were not interested in or ready for coaching. The person who had taken on her previous assignments did not want to give them up, so the premature coach was out of a job. She wasted a great amount of organizational resources before doing a needs assessment or letting coaching evolve with demand.

So don't give up your day job or spend a lot of time and money on infrastructure before doing some market research within your business if you are an internal consultant or in your target markets if you are an external coach. Then build your infrastructure for your coaching practice based on what you learn from your research.

Office Space

Much executive coaching takes place at the client's office or over the phone. You may also arrange for your clients to meet you at your office. Depending on the degree to which you practice onsite, through telecommunications, or in your office, your infrastructure requirements will by necessity be very different. When distance coaching is the only option given the geographic location of the client, it is entirely appropriate to communicate by phone, videoconferencing, e-mail, or Web dialogues. But consider the overwhelming importance of body language in reading and understanding each others' messages, both direct and indirect.

There is very little reliable data on the relationship between coaching practices and outcomes. Rather than being able to depend on research findings, we often have to rely on experience, our own and others', to decide how to interact with clients. Based on my own experience, as well as that of many other coaches with whom I exchange best practices on an informal basis, I have concluded that face-to-face sessions have much more impact than coaching by phone or other electronic means. This appears to be especially the case when the focus is on developing the coachee as a leader through improved communications skills, passion, presence, trust, interpersonal interaction, influence, team dynamics, and related leadership capabilities and styles. It may have less importance when coaching goals are associated with content knowledge, business planning, issues not related to people, and the implementation of business plans.

Unlike a counseling or therapy session, which mostly involves talking in a relaxed atmosphere, executive coaching usually requires a conference table at which you and your client can review materials, write plans, practice conducting meetings, or explore new approaches to complex work problems. If you meet in your client's office, reserve a conference room if the personal office does not provide enough privacy and space. If it is appropriate or convenient for your clients to meet you outside their own facilities, you must have a meeting space available in your office or access to another site as needed. If you are accustomed to sitting behind your desk talking with people at a distance, consider rethinking your role and design your space so you can work with your client as an equal rather than sitting across the desk in the chair of power. You can also find another location conducive to coaching. One alternative is to use a colleague's office or rent space on an hourly or daily basis.

Whether you meet at your client's office, your office, or another space, you will need certain equipment. At a minimum, you'll need a computer and printer. If you do not know in advance which tools or materials you'll use during coaching, carry a file of materials either in hard copy or, more conveniently, electronically. A multimedia laptop is useful for recording and playback, showing video demonstrations or instructional programs, videoconferencing others into the coaching session, or accessing the multitude of resources available on the Web. A portable digital projector that connects to your memory device or laptop makes it easy to share materials, videos, or Web-based resources in a group setting.

Needless to say, your office serves many other purposes besides providing a location for coaching sessions. Design your space based on how you plan to use it as well as your own preferences. If you will spend a lot of time in your office, especially consider investing in ergonomic furniture and equipment such as a headset, speaker phone, soundproofing, appropriate lighting, background music, and a style and color scheme that make you comfortable and yet ready to work.

If you plan to work out of your home office, there are many considerations to take into account. Check the local regulations for using residential property for business purposes. You may need to register your business locally. Home mail delivery is sometimes inadequate for large packages and deliveries requiring a signature or protected drop-off space. The normal life going on around you in your home can make it difficult to concentrate and may interrupt your concentration — or even worse, a coaching session.

Many coaches love working from home: no commute, no need to go anywhere at any time of day or night. Other coaches need to get away from the house to have a balanced life. Consider not only your preferences, but also the implications, costs, and benefits of a home versus an external office.

Data and File Management

Effective executive coaching often requires a great deal of data for each coaching case. You need an easy-to-use, efficient system to store and access that information. Each coaching project should have its own file, organized in a standard way that makes it easy to plan, track progress, maintain communication, and reference at a later date. Minimally, each professional executive coaching project file should include:

- Contact information
- Contracts and agreements
- A project plan and timetable
- A record of client contacts and activities
- Assessment data and reports
- Meeting notes
- Action plans
- A list or copy of resource materials you have shared with the client
- A record of measured results of the coaching
- A copy of correspondence associated with the coaching
- Project budget, resource allocation, and a record of invoicing and payments
- Project reports, conclusions, and follow-up notes

You also need a written policy and agreement with each client about protecting, maintaining, and dealing with the coaching file during and at the end of the project. Check the applicable laws and professional guidelines for your region and professional affiliations and establish and document your file management polices and procedures accordingly.

Finance Management

A comprehensive computer-based financial management system will help you process, track, and generate reports on the money coming in and out of your practice. If you travel extensively, this system or a bookkeeper can save you many hours each month dealing with the often voluminous records required for reimbursable travel expenses. Many large organizations prefer or require you to conduct your financial transactions with them electronically, including billing, fund transfers, reports, and associated exchanges. Tax agencies may also require you to process regular reports and payments electronically. If you set up your practice as an entity with employees, even if you are the only employee, you will have to submit regular payroll reports and payments electronically.

Whether electronic or manual, done by you or in collaboration with a professional bookkeeper or accountant, you need a system that can handle financial complexity without requiring a lot of your time. Many professionals don't want to pay others for their services and prefer to do it all themselves. Even if you like to do your own accounting, tax preparation, or other noncoaching activities, consider how much money you could be making if you were doing coaching instead of paperwork or financial reports.

Technology and Your Virtual Office

Wherever you are, your virtual office should be available to you. Your executive coaching clients and their organizations have high expectations of your accessibility and responsiveness. Waiting to get back to your actual office to check voicemail, reply to e-mail, or access and forward documents is often just not good enough to meet those expectations. Gain a competitive edge with a PDA, Web-linked laptop, cell phone, and access to voicemail, e-mail, text messages, the Web, and your file of materials. It is a challenging balancing act to remain accessible and responsive while setting limits and maintaining privacy when you are not working. To establish a balance that meets both your professional and personal needs, set ground rules with clients about when you will and won't be accessible.

If you are a road warrior spending a great deal of time driving from client to client, be aware of the dangers, and in many cases the illegality, of using your electronic devices while driving. The U.S. National Highway Traffic Safety Administration (NHTSA) reported that in 2005 close to a million drivers, or approximately 10% of everyone driving at any given moment during daylight hours were using a handheld phone. Whether a cell phone is handheld or hands-free, cognitive distraction is significant enough to negatively affect a driver's performance (www.nhtsa.dot.gov). Most of us also know what it's like to be on the road next to a driver who is distracted by a phone or electronic device—don't be one of them. Client accessibility is not worth the risk of a causing an accident, or even death.

Access to Knowledge and Information from Outside Your Practice

Your practice should include a view of the world around you: best practices, what works in leadership and coaching, stories, examples, and varied approaches to achieve business results. The professional executive coach should not be a lone ranger, using personal experience as the only source of knowledge and reference. As the world of work and the discipline of coaching evolve, you must have access to information and databases that will help your clients stay up-to-date—on leaders, organizations, and the current and forecasted business environment in which clients develop and execute their plans. Information and data sources come in many forms, including normative assessment devices; blogs of leaders sharing their challenges and solutions; books of best practices in leadership, coaching, teamwork, communication, and managing change; and research reports on emerging trends in scenario planning and strategy implementation. Avoid the all-too-common trap of wearing blinders, drawing solely from what you personally know rather than the knowledge and experience of other experts.

It takes an investment of time and systems to collect, update, and make accessible the knowledge base that is useful to you and your clients. But that investment pays off in better service and increased demand when you offer a value proposition based not only on what you know but on the knowledge your clients can access. The Appendix lists many resources I suggest and that have been recommended by other experts in the field.

How to Manage Coaching Projects

Figure 4.1 presents a seven-step process for customizing a project management system to your own approach and style, and to each individual leader you coach. The process starts before coaching actually begins, with scoping and exploring the project, and ends as you work with partners to monitor and support results during and after the coaching.

Scope and Explore the Project

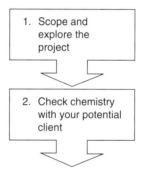

People in a variety of roles contact executive coaches about a prospective client: leaders seeking coaches, their bosses, a human resources professional in their organization, or even a spouse or friend. Your perspective on the coaching need or opportunity will be biased by your initial contact's point of view. To develop a better understanding of the situation and the system in which the coaching may take place, it is important to talk with all of the key stakeholders and partners involved in the coaching. Begin by talking with each of these people individually, and then bring them together to agree on coaching goals.

For example, a potential coachee may tell you that he is a high-potential player in the organization and is seeking coaching to position himself for the next level of leadership and advance his career. The human resources contact fills you in on the strengths, weaknesses, and circumstances that led the boss to encourage this executive to seek coaching as part of his development plan. The boss herself says that the coachee is a key player, describes perform-ance problems, and explains that the ways senior management perceives the coachee are limiting his career opportunities in the organization. An internal coach who worked with this leader in the past year tells you that the leader is just placating his boss without showing any willingness to try anything new.

A phone call or face-to-face meeting with each of the key peo-ple involved will provide multiple perspectives that help you gain an initial sense of what is going on. Is the prospective coachee ready for productive coaching? Is he in a situation that will pro-vide support? You will also begin to establish possible initial goals for the coaching. Coaching is not the right answer for a situation just because you are being asked to do it.

When you consult a surgeon about a medical problem, she will analyze your condition to decide if you are a good candidate for surgery. If you are having marital difficulties and ask a divorce attorney how to make arrangements for your children, he may decide you should file for joint custody. And when a leader or orga-nization comes to you as an executive coach to request coaching, you will be inclined to assess readiness and establish goals for the coaching. The surgeon may not consider a change of lifestyle and eating habits as the best way to alleviate symptoms. The divorce attorney may not recommend alternative approaches to dealing with the special needs of the children that may be the major cause of marital strife. Likewise, an executive coach may assume that coaching is the right answer to deal with a leader's problems with-out considering that the problems may have more to do with the organizational system in which the leader works.

So don't automatically assume that coaching is the solution. Rather, your first step should be to scope out the situation, assess the opportunities and problems, and determine if coaching is an appropriate part of an intervention to achieve the desired objec-tives. Developing the coachee will have little impact if other major problems need to be resolved before, or in conjunction with, the coaching. Perhaps the organization needs total restructuring — coaching one of its leaders will not accomplish that. Or the leader's boss may stand in the way of success. Consider organizational politics, which may be putting the leader in the untenable situation of pleasing multiple constituents who cannot agree on priorities.

The focus of the initial conversations should be on the system within which the prospective coachee works. Begin with open-ended questions, and listen actively to encourage each person to tell you more until you exhaust the different categories that need to be explored. Maintain an organizational systems perspective using the following checklist to guide your initial exploration:

Coaching Project Scoping Topics
- The organization's values, vision, mission, and strategy
- The individual's role in leading and contributing to the accomplishment of the organization's strategic and tactical objectives
- Current and recent organizational performance and factors that may contribute to that performance
- Areas in which the individual needs to be competent to succeed in his or her current role
- The individual's current and recent performance
- Current areas of competence
- Gaps in the individual's competence and performance
- Special goals, standards, or opportunities that are especially important now or will be in the near future
- Opportunities for the individual to take on new or expanded responsibilities
- Other factors that may help or hinder the individual's current performance or future advancement
- New responsibilities that the individual has or will be taking on
- The individual's personal career objectives, job satisfaction, and beliefs about him/herself and the organization
- The individual's relationships with key people at work

- The dynamics and effectiveness of teams that the individual leads or belongs to
- Any factors outside of work that affect the individual and his or her performance at work
- Recent or forecasted events or conditions in the organization's industry and business environment
- Recent activities, initiatives, and consulting or coaching relationships in which the individual has been involved or that are relevant to the situation in which coaching would take place

Check Your Chemistry with Your Potential Client

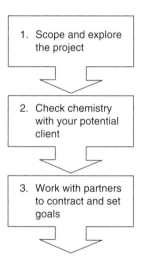

Interpersonal chemistry is an emotional thing. Do you, your client, and the key people involved in the coaching feel that you can all work well together? Will your values, assumptions, style, and preferences mesh for the benefit of the coachee? To figure out if you have the right chemistry, you and your coachee need time to discover how each of you think, feel, behave, and respond to each other. If the coaching will be face-to-face, meet your client in person to check your chemistry. If coaching will be done remotely, then the medium you choose may be sufficient to determine the quality of your interaction. The key is to simulate the situations in which you will coach.

Talk to your coachee about what is important to each of you in your working relationship. Get to know each other by doing some preliminary coaching. Above all, you must both be open and honest about the degree to which you fit each other's preferences and priorities. At the end of the chemistry-check conference, talk about how each of you perceives the match. Rather than asking if the chemistry is there, I find it more helpful to talk about ways in which there is a good fit. Also discuss challenges to overcome were you to work together. I have rarely found a prospective coachee able or willing to admit a lack of chemistry. So plan a follow-up discussion or e-mail to check whether you both feel you could work well together.

Prospective clients who are interviewing more than one potential coach may feel more comfortable relaying their decision to you through an intermediary. A human resources professional or the client's boss is often chosen for this purpose.

When a potential coachee's boss, human resources professional, or anyone else will be an integral part of the coaching, you must conduct an appropriate chemistry with that person, too. In your initial meetings with these individuals, include in the agenda a discussion about how they work, how you work, and finally, how each of you views the match.

As professional executive coaches we must accept our own emotional triggers, stylistic tendencies, strengths, and priorities. We must be as strong, competent, and unbiased as possible. But no matter how much we prepare ourselves, we cannot be good coaches for every person and situation. The chemistry check is not one-sided It is for you to decide if you are the best fit for the client, as well as for the client to decide if you are the best fit. If you do not like to work with self-centered, arrogant, slow-paced, or manipulative people, then you owe it to your client and yourself to help such a person find a coach who will be more supportive and positive. If you believe strongly that a coachee's boss or board needs to be involved in the coaching but a prospective client is not able or interested to make that happen, consider guiding the coachee and the organization to someone else.

Work with the Partners in the Coaching Project
to Contract and Set Goals

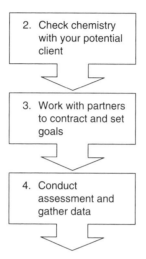

As an executive coach, you work in partnership with the coachee, his or her manager, and the organization to establish the goals of the coaching. Then you collaborate with these partners to manage the coaching and achieve the agreed-on goals.

EXTERNAL COACHING   If you are an external coach, there are several types of contracts, formal and informal, which you may want to establish with your coaching partners. Each contract may involve different members of the partnership. The formal coaching contract is typically executed in writing between you or your firm and the coachee's organization. One of the first things to do is to determine who represents the client organization for the purposes of coming to agreement for the contract. Sometimes it is the coachee or the coachee's manager; other times it may be the human resources professional who coordinates coaching or a representative from the purchasing or legal department.

Some organizations prefer you to submit a proposal or draft contract for them to review, edit, and sign. Others use a standard contracting template or provide you with a contract for your review. When you are the one submitting the contract, seek counsel from an attorney regarding the terms, conditions, and form of a template agreement from which to build a contract for each project. For complex projects and contracts, consider having your attorney review the terms of those agreements.

Other client organizations avoid contracting altogether and assume that your coaching will be driven by an informal verbal agreement. Often the person with whom you verbally contract may not represent the points of view of others in the organization, will remember things differently than you do, or end up changing roles or even leaving the organization during the course of the coaching. Although a complex contract is rarely necessary, a basic written agreement setting forth the terms and conditions of your work will minimize later confusion and disagreement. The following is a sample of the terms and conditions to define in your agreement:

- The client organization, coachee, and official representative of the client organization for your project.
- The coaching firm and/or coach for the project.
- Your deliverables as coach: length of the project, number and length of coaching sessions, how the coaching will take place (face-to-face, by phone, other), assessments, reports, support meetings, goals and measures of success, and so on.
- The coaching process: premeetings, involvement of the coachee's boss, human resources, and others, communication between coaching sessions, and so on.
- Involvement and support from the client organization: facilities, equipment, administrative support, survey administration, and so on.
- Fees and payment terms.
- Reimbursement for travel and other project-related expenses.

- Confidentiality and management of proprietary information, including file management.
- Terms for scheduling, rescheduling, cancellation of meetings, and termination of the project.

INTERNAL COACHING   As an internal coach, you probably already have a contract as an employee of the organization. Although a formal agreement may not be necessary for coaching work that is significantly different from your typical responsibilities, an informal communication within the organization spelling out your role is beneficial. Specify such issues as:

- How to deal with information discussed in the coaching
- How much time you will invest in the coaching
- How your coaching activities should be evaluated in your performance reviews
- Which external resources will support you and the coaching process

In addition to the informal communication about your internal coaching work, for each coaching project the coaching partners must agree on details of the coaching and how they will interact during the project. Informal or not, putting this agreement in writing will increase the likelihood that all parties understand and agree to it. Include specific information regarding such issues as:

- Keeping each other informed
- Handling assessment and 360-degree results
- The role of the coachee's manager in supporting the coaching
- The availability of the human resources representative during the coaching project
- Dealing with issues of trust, respect, openness, boundaries, and conflict

Conduct the Assessment and Gather Data

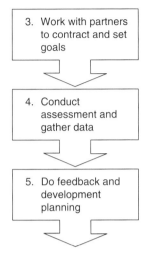

The goals established in Phase 3 of the coaching process will help you decide what assessments and data to collect about any of the following:

- The coachee, including tendencies, habits, interests, strengths, weaknesses, history, how viewed by others
- The coachee's relationships at work
- Teams that the coachee belongs to or leads
- The organization
- The organization's business environment

As an example, if one of the goals of the coaching is to build the coachee's leadership presence, you may need to establish how her presence is currently perceived, her tendency and current level of self-confidence and communication skills, and the organization's cultural values for leadership.

Your assessment and data-gathering plan starts with a review and analysis of the information currently available. If you determine that further data are necessary, develop and implement a plan to collect, analyze, report on, provide feedback on, and utilize the data to answer the seven following questions:

1. What results should the coachee and his or her team and organization be accomplishing now and in the future?
2. How should those results be accomplished?
3. To what degree and in what ways are they currently being accomplished? How will they be accomplished in the future?
4. How satisfied are the coachee and his or her key constituents with the past, current, and projected results and the ways those results are or will be accomplished?
5. What are the coachee's and his or her team's or organization's current abilities, supporting factors, barriers to, and likelihood of accomplishing the desired results?
6. What is the coachee's and his or her team's or organization's capacity to improve those abilities and supporting factors and remove the barriers? Are they likely to accomplish the desired results?
7. What would it take to accomplish the desired results?

The primary objectives in this phase of the coaching process are to analyze any existing data and conduct new assessments and data gathering to answer these seven questions. Data collection must be done in ways that support the coaching without any negative impact on the coachee or the organization. Use the following guidelines to accomplish these objectives:

- To the extent possible, inform or have the coachee or other members of the coaching partnership inform people in the organization about the assessment and data-gathering plan.
- Have the coaching partners obtain support for and permission from people before involving them in assessment and data gathering.
- Implement the plan in an ethical, professional, and respectful way to maximize the validity and reliability of the assessment results and data; treat people and the organization positively and professionally.

- Refine the coaching goals and plan based on a shared review of assessment and data results; follow the agreed-upon guidelines for coaching and confidentiality.
- Establish quantitative and qualitative measures of success for the coaching.

Conduct Feedback and Development Planning

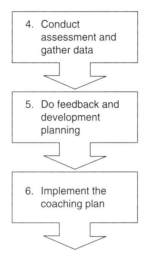

Executive coaching usually involves one or two feedback and development-planning sessions. These sessions increase coachees' understanding of what they are doing and the factors that affect their performance and future potential in the organization. A related feedback goal is to help the coachee become more aware and understand the extent to which their behavior and other factors are affecting the achievement of results. Development-planning sessions assist the organization in understanding what the coachees are doing, factors that are helping or hindering their effectiveness, their impact on the organization, and how to increase their ability to contribute to the organization. Feedback and development planning allows coachees to "own" what they are doing and become aware of evidence-based factors affecting their performance and organizational results. The following steps will guide the feedback and development planning process:

1. If you have not yet met with the coachee to set expectations and agree on the purpose, content, and process of feedback and development planning, do so prior to the first feedback session.

   Guidelines:
   - Discuss and put in writing a list of questions the coachee and organization want answered by the assessment and feedback data. Also document the decisions to be made as a result of the answers to those questions.
   - If the organization has a standard process or guidelines for feedback and development planning, apply that process or integrate it in with your own.

2. Ensure an understanding within the coaching partnership regarding the confidentiality of feedback and how, if at all, members of the partnership will be involved in the process. Also spell out whether all members receive a report or any of the data findings.

3. Report on the feedback data. Provide a guide for the coachee on how to analyze the data. Give the coachee the assignment of responding to the questions to be answered from the data.

   Guidelines:
   - Customize the reports based on the learning and communication styles of the coachee. Some people accept and understand feedback if presented as pictures and graphs, others as tables and text, and still others as a series of questions and answers.
   - Whenever possible, rather than providing the answers you derive from the data, present it in a form coachees can analyze to draw their own conclusions. This is a balancing act along a continuum. At one end, you provide raw data that require a great deal of analysis on the part of coachees. At the other end, you draw the essential conclusions and implications from the data yourself. By analyzing the data themselves and coming to their own conclusions, coachees are more likely to own the results and act on them.

4. Schedule two or three feedback and development sessions. Session length will depend on the quantity and complexity of the data and the ease or difficulty the coachee will have in receiving and internalizing the information. A typical session lasts two to three hours.

5. Conduct the first feedback and development planning session.

   Guidelines:
   - Walk through the data and help the coachee understand them enough to be able to analyze them alone before the second session.
   - Ask the coachee to draft answers to the questions you established in Step 1 of the feedback and development planning process. To help you prepare for the second meeting, the coachee should send you a data analysis and any answers to the questions beforehand.

6. Conduct the second feedback and development planning session.

   Guidelines:
   - Review the coachee's analyses and answers as well as your own. Guide coachees in comparing their own view of the data to yours. Answer, or review the answers to the questions, as planned.
   - You may also use this session to generate a development/coaching plan. Work with the coachee to develop the plan if you have time do so. If there is not enough time to work on the plan in this session, schedule a third.
   - Typically a development plan includes the strengths, weaknesses, opportunities, and constraints of the coachee, his or her teams, the organization, and other factors on which data were collected. The plan should also include development goals for the coachee, teams, and organization. It should define which of those goals to address through coaching versus other means.
   - When 360-degree feedback has been gathered and it is appropriate, prepare the coachee to go back to the feedback

sources to share learning from the feedback and thank them for their participation. Discuss how the coachee can explore ways to apply the learning with each person who provided feedback.

7. Conduct a third feedback and development planning session, if needed.

   Guidelines:
   • When a third session is called for, work to complete the development/coaching plan if necessary. Debrief any conclusions and plans developed in the second session. Ask the coachee to prepare a summary for the other members of the coaching partnership and send you a draft for feedback and edits.

8. Meet with the coaching partnership to help the coachee share learning from the assessment and data and suggested goals for development.

   Guidelines:
   • Prior to this meeting, agree with your coachee on the degree to which you are free to use your own judgment on sharing details of the assessment and data.
   • Begin the meeting by setting the agenda and ground rules, including:
     —A reminder of the confidentiality agreement, the goals of the assessment and data gathering, and the questions to be answered;
     —A description of the assessments and data collected, including process and sources;
     —The coachee's reactions to and insights derived from the results;
     —Specific goals and guidelines for the coaching;
     —The roles of partnership members during the coaching; and
     —Coaching schedule and follow-up.
   • Don't lead the meeting—help your coachee to do it. Make sure your coachee prepares a summary handout of the

assessments and data, an analysis, reactions, conclusions, coaching goals, and the support required from the coaching partnership. Assist the coachee in reviewing the data collected, the analysis, and the answers to the questions for which the data were collected. Facilitate a discussion of the findings, the reactions of the other members of the partnership, and a consensus on moving forward with the coaching and other developmental activities.

Implement the Coaching Plan

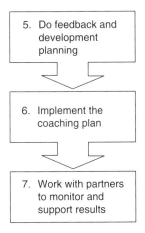

As a result of the assessment, data gathering, feedback, and development planning, you need to "recontract" with the coachee regarding goals, the timetable, and how you will work together to accomplish the newly defined coaching goals. Help the coachee put together a more detailed plan on what you will work on during and between each session. Use a coaching timetable like the one in Table 4.2 to specify goals, the order in which to tackle the goals, and how many sessions to dedicate to each.

Establish expectations on what you will do together during the coaching sessions and what you and the coachee will do individually in between. Include working on goals, communicating

144

Table 4.2 Sample Coaching Timetable

	SESSION									
GOALS	1	2	3	4	5	6	7	8	9	10
Develop greater "executive presence"	→	→	→							
Hold people more accountable			→	→	→	→				
Develop and communicate a strategic plan				→	→	→	→	→		
Develop career goals and work with mentors to move toward those goals								→	→	→

with each other, measuring and monitoring progress, and involving others in the implementation of the plan. For coachees who prefer or can benefit from more structure as described in Chapter 1, establish a standard agenda for each coaching session. Here is an example:

- Discuss what's new in the coachee's work situation.
- Review what the coachee has done since the last session to accomplish coaching goals.
- Work on the coaching goal(s) scheduled for the current coaching session (e.g., practice new skills, develop strategic plans, analyze factors affecting team performance, prepare for presentations).

- Agree on assignments and activities to complete before the next coaching session.
- Plan the agenda for the next session.
- Debrief this coaching session for learning opportunities and ways to maximize the utility of future coaching sessions.

Whenever possible, there should be contact between you and the coachee between sessions. To continue the evidence-based nature of the coaching, observe the coachee on the job to monitor and reinforce progress or provide further feedback. Don't assume your coachee will be able to apply what you discuss and practice during your sessions. Instead, make the coaching a continuous process. The follow-up between sessions is especially important when the coaching involves changing habits or developing new ways of thinking and feeling. Because progress in these areas is usually gradual and incremental, follow-up will help to reinforce small improvements and catch any regression before it goes very far. Set a standard that you and the coachee will phone, e-mail, or meet informally between coaching sessions. Encourage the coachee and manage the coaching to meet that standard.

Many coaches, especially new ones, allow the coaching session to be driven by free association and whatever is happening in the coachee's work or mind that day. While some openness and spontaneity in the coaching agenda can be productive, I have found that a more goal-driven approach increases the likelihood of achieving the contracted results. The safer environment of the coaching relationship makes it tempting for both coach and coachee to slip into counseling and an open dialogue. Given the definition of professional executive coaching on which this book is based, implementation of the coaching plan should be driven by specific goals to build the coachee's leadership capabilities and achieve targeted organizational results. This is the priority, not discussing what is on the coachee's mind or what the coach has been thinking about or reading since the last session.

Work with the Coaching Partners to Monitor and Support the Coaching

Too often in executive coaching situations, once the coachee receives feedback and specific goals are established, coach and coachee are left to their own devices to let the magic of coaching do its thing. In a true partnership among the coach, coachee, coachee's boss, human resources, and other key members of the organization, all the partners are involved in the coaching until it is complete. They maximize success by continuously monitoring coaching progress and providing ongoing support. A successful coaching outcome depends on quantitative and qualitative measures of success, geared to the development of the coachee as a leader and the accomplishment of organizational results.

Whenever possible, the coachee's boss should also be providing coaching and shaping the coachee's positive practices based on observation and feedback on the job. Over the course of the coaching, the boss and coachee should schedule about an hour each month to monitor and support the coaching agenda.

During a coaching project, the coaching partnership should meet as a group at least four times with the following goals:

1. Scope out and agree on the coaching goals and ground rules.
2. Review the findings and implications of the assessment and data feedback and development planning.
3. Monitor the progress of the coaching, often at about two-thirds of the way through the coaching.
4. When the coaching is complete, review progress, recognize success, develop new goals for continued development, and

147

agree on ways to support the coachee in holding the gain and making further progress.

Either you or another member of the partnership should document and distribute the agenda, minutes, and action items from each of these meetings.

HOW TO OPTIMIZE LEARNING FROM PROFESSIONAL AND PEER SUPERVISION

Supervision is a cornerstone of most professional practices. Whether in executive coaching, law, education, mental health, accounting, or other disciplines, we should confidentially review what we do with our peers and others who are more experienced. Such a review provides greater objectivity, quality control, and continuous learning. It is especially important for a new executive coach. You owe it to yourself, your clients, and the evolving field of professional executive coaching to share your coaching challenges and opportunities with other new coaches as well as tenured professionals in the field.

Professional Supervision

As a new executive coach, it is most beneficial to hire a professional supervisor with the experience you lack and the supervision skills to help you serve your clients and learn from your initial coaching cases. Professional supervision is also especially valuable when you offer new services or work with unfamiliar client situations.

Use your network to find a supervisor, and be selective. Review resumes and talk with references as well as people who know prospective supervisors to get a sense of their work and style. Interview candidates as you might interview a primary-care physician, potential employee, or manager. Remember how you learn. In the same way that a client should select a coach with a background and style that matches the client's needs and preferences, you should select a supervisor who can help you learn according to your preferences and serve as a role model for the kinds of coaching you want to do.

Peer Supervision

It is very easy to fall into the trap of coaching on autopilot once you have gained experience and confidence. Without stepping back to consider the unique needs of each coaching situation, many coaches use standard protocols and processes and make assumptions about what clients need, how they learn, and how they accomplish their objectives. Peer supervision is a valuable form of continuing education, support, and coaching. A small group of coaches, typically two to eight, may meet on a regular basis (at least once a month). Meetings may take place in person, by conference call, on the Internet, or through other forms of communication. The group shares goals for learning and support as well as ground rules for confidentiality, dialogue, respect, and other guidelines. Peer supervision can be self-led or directed by a professional facilitator.

Get the Most out of Supervision

Whether you hire a professional supervisor or join a peer supervision group, the value of the supervision depends on factors similar to the ones that determine coaching success. Agree with your peers on the goals of the supervision and sign a contract on how it is to be conducted. Include agenda, content, process, agreements for any financial remuneration, frequency and duration of meetings, communication between sessions, and a method for measuring the supervision's success. In the same way that coaching may take place face-to-face or can be accomplished through other means, decide on the form of supervision based on its goals, content, the feasibility of meeting in person, and your communication and learning style.

Observing and analyzing how you interact with your supervisor can be as much of a learning opportunity as what you discuss in your sessions. As an example, if you have difficulty admitting what you don't know or tend to monopolize the supervision by talking instead of asking questions, you may need to change how you coach to be more open to learning from and with your client. For supervision to provide you with optimum learning, step back on a regular basis to analyze what you are doing and its implications for you as a coach. Process what you do in supervision as it happens, not just at the end. Supervision offers you the perfect opportunity to develop more empathy for your clients by experiencing what they go through in coaching. You have to be vulnerable, ask for help, focus on goals, and manage your own learning and success. Supervision can heighten understanding, appreciation, and support for your clients as you experience the challenges and opportunities of your own learning.

CONDUCTING RESEARCH AND PUBLISHING ARTICLES ABOUT YOUR COACHING

There is an interesting phenomenon that I have seen in many executive coaches as well as experiencing it myself. I suspect it is as true for other professionals in applied practice as it is for executive coaches. Most executive coaches like the action-oriented, practical, and interpersonal nature of coaching. They may be doers more than thinkers, inclined to implement a process instead of researching it. Organizations can be similar. Few of them that hire executive coaches are willing to invest the time and money to systematically evaluate the outcomes of the coaching, the factors related to the outcomes, and the effectiveness of and satisfaction with the process used to achieve those outcomes.

Although our intuition or gut impression tells us that certain ways of coaching, situations, people, organizations, and coaches get better results, I am not aware of any controlled research to demonstrate a consistent pattern associated with desirable outcomes. Most executive coaches are not interested in or capable of conducting controlled outcome studies of what they do. Even so, each of us should gather data from which we can learn as a professional discipline. For example, if all of us were to track how individuals and organizations define coaching outcomes, and monitor some objective measures of these outcomes for individual coaching cases and across similar and different cases, we may begin to identify patterns for researchers to test in more controlled studies. We can also maintain blind records of assessment findings by coding our coaching cases, including goals, methods, and results as evaluated by the coaching partnership. With these data, we could begin to track patterns to feed into a shared database. Client confidentiality would be protected as we analyze the data to discover patterns to guide the services we provide to our clients.

As professionals in a relatively new discipline, we can and should begin by sharing case studies of our work while protecting client confidentiality. We also can benefit simply by sharing what and how we think about executive coaching from our many professional backgrounds. Currently we expend too much energy worrying if coaches who publish their ideas and stories have the best academic credentials or whether those in influential positions in the field agree with our points of view. It is too early to limit what we publish—not that such a time will ever come. We owe it to each other and to our clients to conduct an open exchange of ideas and case examples, especially in this linked world of Internet communication.

Do everything you must to protect the confidentiality of your clients. Report your ideas and stories in clear, concise, and responsible ways. Join with others with similar and different backgrounds to build databases of what you do, what seems to work, and how clients and colleagues view your work. Demonstrate humility and interdependence as you study and report on your work. Share it with everyone who could benefit from what you have learned: leaders, would-be-leaders, human resources professionals, coaches, consultants, researchers, and students.

BUILDING COMMUNITY SERVICE INTO YOUR PRACTICE

My wife and I grew up in families whose members dedicated a certain percentage of their time to providing professional services at little or no cost to the communities in which they worked. My father was a professional musician. Each week he gave some of his time to directing a chorus that donated all of its performance fees to a scholarship fund for music students. My parents wrote and staged musicals together to raise funds for local nonprofit organizations. My wife's grandfather was a dentist who provided dental services at a free clinic one day a week.

As members of our local, business, and world communities, professional executive coaches have the opportunity to make a significant difference without personal gain: to coach leaders of small nonprofit organizations, religious and government leaders, the disabled and special-needs community, and up-and-coming high-school and college students.

Rather than simply offering your time to any leaders or organizations who would find it difficult if not impossible to pay for your services, blend your professional and personal passions by donating your services to causes that have a special place in your heart. As professional executive coaches, we have a unique opportunity to help leaders who can influence areas particularly important to us. If you believe strongly in the work or principles of a certain religious group, offer to coach its professional and lay leaders. If you have a strong commitment to a political party or initiative, coach their leaders. If you are concerned about an environmental, geopolitical, economic, societal, cultural, or other cause, volunteer your coaching services at little or no cost.

There are two challenges associated with volunteering a portion of your professional time to community service. First, it is just as important to follow the professional and ethical guidelines of executive coaching in these situations. Your pro bono coachees deserve the same high level of service as do your paying clients. Second, it is difficult to set limits on your pro bono contributions. It may not be easy to say no when a pro bono client refers a colleague for further voluntary services. When we become involved in causes, many of us find it easy to donate to them in other forms. This is not a bad thing—it simply requires a purposeful balancing of time and resources between earning a living and making a more satisfying and meaningful impact on the world in which we live.

Transitioning into Executive Coaching from Other Specialty Fields

If you are coming into the professional practice of executive coaching from another specialty field, you bring with you potential strengths and weaknesses. The baggage you carry includes not only knowledge and expertise but also biases, limitations, blind spots, and habits that can interfere with effectively serving your executive coaching clients.

Executive coaches come from a number of fields, including mental health, business management, organization development and management consulting, personal/life coaching, and internal human resources. Many people who want to enter executive coaching come from two or more of these specialties.

Depending on your training or background, you have a unique set of strengths and potential barriers to take into account as you transition into executive coaching. Mental health professionals often need to let go of their medical models, problem-solving processes, and orientation to serve as reflectors of emotions.

Business managers who move into the coaching arena are often less than sensitive to emotional intelligence and the psychological or organizational-systems perspectives so critical to executive coaching. Organization development and management consultants sometimes want to change the system when, as executive coaches, their primary focus must be on the individual leader or group of leaders within the context of the organization. Personal/life coaches may be unfamiliar with the complexities of business, leadership, and organizational dynamics and unable to step beyond the individual's needs and priorities. Human resources professionals who have worked in organizations often need to break loose of the cultural norms and hierarchical pressures that can prevent them from providing honest feedback and objective views of a coachee's organization. Other specialty backgrounds — career coaching, communications, developmental coaching, medical, speech and language, religious, community service, political, financial management, sports — can all contribute to the field of executive coaching.

Don't fall into the trap of defining yourself by your former specialty. Make sure you don't limit your coaching strategies based solely on your specialty training, expertise, or perspective. Whether you come to executive coaching from a background in business, human resources, life coaching, or another specialty, apply the suggestions in this chapter to leveraging your strengths and overcoming the limitations of your previous education, training, professional disciplines, and mindset.

TRANSITIONING FROM MENTAL HEALTH PROFESSIONS

Mental health professionals are trained to assess, treat, sustain, and support people's mental health. Some focus on its physiological and medical aspects; others more on its cognitive, behavioral, interpersonal, and societal sides. Many professionals use a medical model to diagnose and treat mental illness. Others have an approach that has more recently been described as "positive psychology" (Seligman, 2002). They focus less on abnormality and treatment and more on individual differences, strengths, developing potential, and restructuring expectations and the way we think to enhance satisfaction, effectiveness, and the meaning in our life.

Some physicians and other medically oriented mental health professionals concentrate on the brain, physiological and neurochemical problems, and curing or alleviating difficulties through medical means and lifestyle changes. Others are more concerned with the way clients function in their social environment. These practitioners focus on interpersonal and group dynamics and strategies, helping their clients positively affect the system in which they live and work. Depending on your theoretical and practical orientation in mental health, you bring into executive coaching different strengths and limitations.

Strategies for Transitioning from a Mental Health Background

First and foremost, if you think your mental health affiliation is better than other backgrounds for executive coaching, give up this arrogant point of view. Be open to learning from others with different backgrounds and sharing your expertise in exchange. The following strategies will help you transition into executive coaching:

- Focus on what differentiates the individuals you coach without focusing on "abnormalities" or trying to diagnose them.
- Stick to coaching goals associated with building leadership capabilities and achieving organizational results rather than the coachee's personal issues.
- Take the wide perspective of the organizational system to understand what is helping or hindering coachees' success in their business roles.
- Use what you know about psychology, but translate it into everyday and business language rather than employing psychobabble or technical terms.
- Work with coachees as partners to help them discover things about themselves and learn to learn. Don't just teach or tell them what they need to do differently.

- Focus coaching sessions on specific developmental goals rather than free association. The goal of a coaching session is not to provide space and time for coachees to slowly uncover deep therapeutic issues.
- If you do observe, assess, or uncover mental health issues that need therapeutic intervention, help coachees find another resource. You will avoid dual-relationship conflicts or confidentiality dilemmas.
- Be explicit in contracting for the coaching and setting ground rules for your role as a coach, the limits of confidentiality in that role, and limits on confidentiality should you become aware of any impropriety, illegality, or threat to the organization or an individual.
- Learn about and capitalize on a variety of theoretical models and practical approaches. Using a single model or approach may limit the opportunity for the coachee and the organization to learn and achieve results.
- If you have limited your interactions in your mental health practice to your own office, expand your coaching environment to the client's work environment.
- If you have used assessment instruments that are primarily clinical in nature, gain expertise in instruments that have demonstrated validity and reliability beyond the clinical realm.
- If you have set strict limits on any self-disclosure in your clinical practice, consider loosening them. Allowing coaching clients to know a little about you and using yourself as an example may benefit the coaching relationship and help you achieve results.
- Network with other mental health professionals who have transitioned into coaching to approach and resolve issues such as:
  - When and how is it appropriate to go to business dinners with clients?
  - How should you advertise your services?
  - Should you refer to yourself as a doctor or reference your professional license?

- How can you collaborate with human resources professionals and other coaches and consultants to develop your business and manage coaching cases?
- Should you charge or pay referral fees?

If you lack business experience, accept that your mental health background is not enough. You have to become an expert in business, leadership, and other areas.

Use the services of an experienced executive coach for supervision and consultation as you begin your coaching practice and as new and less familiar situations arise.

TRANSITIONING FROM BUSINESS MANAGEMENT

Business managers are trained to focus on business results. Sometimes those results are mostly financial, especially in for-profit companies. In other situations, the results are more mission oriented, as in nonprofit organizations and government agencies. Many business managers and leaders are promoted into management with little or no formal leadership training. If you were formally educated in management many years ago, your education may have focused primarily on traditional functions and models of business management. It may have lacked a depth of understanding about leadership, leadership development, and specific areas such as emotional intelligence that have more recently been found to be critical for effective leadership.

Business management training and experience often produces a traditional focus on financial results, goal achievement, or command and control. If this is your background, you will need significant retraining to shift to a more balanced, evidence-based, and systemic approach to leadership. Experts on management and leadership effectiveness with a balance of transactional and transformational leadership (Burns, 1978) are best prepared to transition into executive coaching, as are coaching managers (Hunt & Weintraub, 2002).

Strategies for Transitioning from a Business Management Background

Even if you are well educated in the theories and practical applications of psychology, management, organization development, and coaching, there are several major challenges you may need to overcome. Here are some strategies to help you:

- If your primary coaching experience has been with people you have managed, develop other sources of influence beyond legitimate authority (such as expertise and charisma).
- As a manager who coaches direct reports, you are the one who sets business goals and priorities. As an executive coach, you do not. Use your business experience, but focus on the coaching goals you have agreed upon with the coachee, boss, and other key constituents in the organization.
- If you have concentrated on the financial arena, expand your focus and expertise to the many other areas of business management: customer, process, and people management; organizational systems; leadership development; communication; and so on.
- If process and relationships have been a minor aside to results, build your base of knowledge and expertise in these other critical aspects of management and leadership, including the economic impact of trust, loyalty, process efficiency, and quality.
- You may be going into executive coaching because you like the people side of business, but have never been good at accomplishing results. You won't be successful as an executive coach until you learn how to achieve tangible business results and can apply that knowledge in your coaching.
- If you are most comfortable managing people to achieve goals and are primarily transactional in your approach, learn about innovation, driving change, and inspiring people to do what may seem to be impossible.
- Autocratic, directional, or instructional styles of management don't work well in executive coaching situations. Learn to help coachees realize and come to their own conclusions about what to do and how to achieve their goals. Good executive

coaches don't do most of the talking or tell their clients what to do. They guide coachees to become more self-aware, realize effective approaches, and implement those approaches on a consistent basis.

- If you like to talk and think you have most of the answers, learn to listen and role-model how to be an explorer to find the answers.
- If you believe that people should be able to change quickly once they are told what to do, learn patience. Realize that the longer people have been doing something one way, or the more they are inclined in that direction, the longer it will take them to shift gears. Remember that they often slip back under pressure. As a coach, you must value and validate the difficulty of leadership development and change.
- Don't go into executive coaching because you don't like to make tough decisions and hold people accountable. Executive coaches make just as many tough decisions as managers. If you don't hold your clients accountable, you won't accomplish very much as a coach.
- If you are most comfortable with numbers and things you can count, balance your measurement of results with the qualitative aspects of leadership and team practices.
- If you are used to selling commodities or technical services, shift the way you market your coaching services to a more consultative approach. Influence others to buy your services by showing them what you can do for them rather than trying to convince them that you are the best.

TRANSITIONING FROM ORGANIZATION DEVELOPMENT OR MANAGEMENT CONSULTING

Organization development and management consultants are trained to evaluate organizational situations, make recommendations for change, and facilitate or implement the needed changes. The focus may be on the system as a whole or on specific aspects in which the consultant has special expertise, such as organizational structure, strategic planning, group dynamics, and information technology. But the primary role of the executive coach is not to transform organizational systems but to develop leaders and help them achieve organizational results.

If you are transitioning into executive coaching from organization development or management consulting, the toughest shift may be to give up the lofty goal of changing the organization. I can't count the number of times I have been asked to coach leaders whom a previous coach tried to convince not to change—it was just the culture that needed changing. When coaches work with organizations over a period of years, they may influence the culture or system through repeated interventions at the individual or team level. And if you do work with a senior executive to change the system, your expertise in organization development is a definite plus. In these cases, the coach functions more like a consultant. But your primary job as executive coach is to build the capability of individuals and teams to work effectively and achieve results within the existing system and culture.

Acquire expertise at the individual and team levels. Your expanded repertoire should include the many areas covered in Chapter 2, including adult learning, motivation, career development, stress management, leadership styles, and team development. Perhaps more important than building your knowledge and expertise on these topics is to change the way you think about organizational situations. You should no longer assume that the reason a leader is unable to achieve results has everything to do with the organization and little to do with the individual. As an executive coach your primary focus needs to be on leaders and their teams, with a secondary focus on systemic factors.

Strategies for Transitioning from an Organization Development or Management Consulting Background

Let go of your need to change the organization, and follow these strategies:

- Fill in any gaps in your knowledge and expertise in individual and team behavior on the organizational level, adult learning, and leadership and team development.
- Replace your organizational report templates with ones focused primarily on the individual leader and leadership teams.
- Think of the individual and the team as systems in themselves within the context of the larger organizational system.
- Be more than an expert evaluator and reporter. The bulk of executive coaching involves patiently helping individuals or leadership teams learn to lead and change to achieve results.
- You are no longer the objective observer who lets others do the work of changing the microskills and habits of individuals and teams. You must expand your skills to help leaders and teams change how they express themselves in speech and body language, think and strategize, react to each other and others outside the team, gain trust and commitment, and make things happen.
- If you are very analytical and less comfortable with the emotional or "human" side of management, use your other strengths until your comfort level increases. If this is simply too much of a stretch for you, work in collaboration with other coaches who balance out your analytical and numbers-driven nature.
- Conversely, you may be going into executive coaching because you are less comfortable with analytical and organizational systems approaches. Fill in any gaps in your knowledge or expertise rather than ignoring this blind spot and letting it get in the way of your coaching.

TRANSITIONING FROM PERSONAL/LIFE COACHING

Personal and life coaches receive training or other preparation from a wide variety of sources. Some complete certification programs on life coaching from recognized organizations with rigorous standards, requiring students to demonstrate their skills through live or online classes and extensive supervised practice. Other personal coaches go through less comprehensive training, supervision, and competency evaluation. Still others perform personal or life coaching as an extension of their counseling, therapy, or consultation practices.

Regardless of your training and background, as an executive coach your biggest shift will be away from thinking of your client as a separate individual. You also need to change your focus from thinking of the coaching goal as helping the individual lead a happier life. Certainly, as an executive coach you care about the individual. As an outgrowth or secondary gain from the executive coaching, your client may gain greater personal effectiveness and fulfillment as a result. But that is not the primary focus of executive coaching.

During executive coaching sessions, the individual or team you coach may often raise their personal needs or life situations. Coming from a personal or life coaching background, you may have a tendency to focus on these personal concerns instead of the stated goals of leadership development and organizational results. Resist spending time on issues that do not contribute directly to the accomplishment of those goals.

Many personal and life coaches believe that, if they can coach individuals or families about personal and life issues, they can automatically coach leaders and teams about leadership and work issues. That would be like a pitching coach thinking he can coach a tennis player or a heart surgeon believing she can perform corneal transplants. Some of the basic skills may be the same but, as I have emphasized throughout this book, a great deal of different knowledge, skills, attributes, and abilities are necessary to do executive coaching. In the same way, without the appropriate training and experience, an executive coach should not perform personal and life coaching without the proper training and preparation.

*Strategies for Transitioning from a Personal
and Life Coaching Background*

If you have no experience working in business or being a leader, gain that experience before going into executive coaching. Here are some other strategies to pursue:

- To avoid any conflicts of interest or ethical dilemmas, separate your personal and life coaching from your executive coaching. As a personal or life coach, your primary clients are your coachees, while as an executive coach your primary client is usually the organization. All too often you will be torn between serving the personal needs and priorities of the individual and those of the organization.
- Before you begin executive coaching, assess yourself against the competencies for executive coaching in Chapter 2. For each area you need to develop, obtain adequate education, training, and supervision.
- When beginning any executive coaching project, do not rely primarily on the input from the individuals or teams you will coach to identify their needs. Work in collaboration with their bosses, human resources professionals, and other key members of the organization to reach a consensus on the coaching goals and measures of success.
- During coaching, divide your time between leadership development and helping the coachee to achieve organizational results. Do not spend any significant time on the coachee's personal issues.
- Use a systems mindset to take into account the multitude of factors affecting the organizational system and business environment in which the coachee works. If you are not proficient in addressing certain factors, seek the advice of others to fill in your gaps in expertise.
- Get professional supervision from an expert in executive coaching or as part of a peer supervision group with experienced coaches.

- If you are used to coaching individuals in your office, go to the organization in which your client works to personally observe the system and meet key people with whom the client interacts.

Transitioning from Internal Human Resources Roles

The field of human resources has undergone significant transformation over the past 10 years. In the past, a primary focus has been on employee relations, the administration of human resource policies and procedures, and working with management to provide services to the individual employee in accordance with governmental regulations and company policy. Today, it is common for the human resources professional to partner with the management team of an organization, function, or business unit.

If you have focused primarily on the more traditional roles of human resources administration, policies and procedures, and services to individual employees, then your move to executive coaching will be major. Your approach to business managers and leaders, and to the organization in which you work, must shift from a transactional one in which you are an internal supplier of administrative and employee relations services to a consultative expert on business management and leadership development. This transition will be difficult within your organization, where people see you in your old role and expect your expertise to be limited to traditional human resources products and services. Whether you already have the skills you need for executive coaching or plan to acquire them through education and training, you may need to move and start fresh in an organization that will respect you for your executive coaching expertise.

If you are a human resources business partner already respected as an expert in business management and leadership and team development, you may be able to shift some or all of your work to executive coaching activities within your organization. Those activities may include direct coaching services and collaboration with other coaches to plan and manage executive coaching.

Excellent references exist with guidelines for human resources professionals on managing executive coaching in organizations (Fitzgerald & Berger, 2002, see especially part III, "Managing Executive Coaching in Organizations"; Valerio & Lee, 2005).

Human resources professionals and human resource business partners have benefits and barriers that external coaches usually do not. It can be a benefit to know the culture and people and have a built-in incentive to help the organization succeed. Your existing relationships with key organizational players may act as either benefits or barriers. A history and knowledge of what has worked, or not, in the organization in the past can save you time, but it may also cause a perception that you are less than open about new ways to succeed. If your existing reputation within the organization aligns with your role as a coach, then it can help. If it does not, it may hurt. It may also throw up a barrier if people associate you with certain members or leaders in the organization.

As an employee of the organization, you share in the benefits of organizational success and the pain of business failures. These factors may affect your neutrality and lead people to question your objectivity. And finally, your associations and commitments to a department or manager through whom you report, plus your obligations and restrictions as an employee, may create additional barriers.

Some human resources professionals have extensive training in the skill areas necessary for executive coaching. Others who see themselves, or are seen by others, as possessing that knowledge do not actually have the required skill set. If you are in the former group, use your background and expertise as you move into executive coaching. If, however, you are in the latter group, move to your strength of humility and gain the expertise you need to coach rather than faking it.

Strategies for Transitioning from Internal Human Resources Roles

Performing executive coaching as an internal human resources professional is not a black-and-white proposition. The question is rarely whether to do it at all; rather, it is a matter of selecting the situations in which you can serve as the most effective coach. In other situations, work with another internal or external coach with different approaches, abilities, or perceptions by people in the organization. Here are some other strategies for human resources professionals transitioning to executive coaching within their current organization:

- Even if you have an educational and experiential background in most of the areas of knowledge and skill needed for executive coaching, be sure to fill in any gaps. Especially if you received your education many years ago, bring yourself up to date on the latest developments in the field.
- If you moved into human resources with little formal education and training in executive coaching skills and haven't gained that expertise in other ways, acquire the skills you need before attempting to do executive coaching.
- If your activities have primarily been in the more traditional administrative and employee relations areas, transition into a human resources business-partner role as an intermediary step to executive coaching. You won't be perceived as a heavyweight and respected by management as a business partner just because you spent years in a human resources administration role. Since it may be very difficult to change that perception in your current organization, consider making the transition into executive coaching elsewhere.
- As an internal employee, you are part of the organizational system. That makes it difficult to be objective about the people and culture with whom you work every day. Human resources professionals are most objective when they first enter an organization. Partner with human resource people new to your organization or with external consultants or coaches. They will help you gain and maintain greater objectivity about your organization as you do executive coaching there.
- To avoid dual relationships or conflicts or interest, avoid coaching people with whom you have a more personal

relationship or who control your performance evaluation, compensation, promotion, or career destiny. Do whatever is necessary to ensure the confidentiality of your executive coaching work. When it would be difficult to remain objective, honest, professional, or confidential, provide references to other internal or external coaches.

- As a member of an organizational culture, you are inclined to accept and participate in the unstated beliefs, assumptions, behaviors, and other norms of which you and others may not be fully aware. One of the greatest values of executive coaching is the ability to step outside and be open to all possibilities. When challenging the status quo is an important part of an executive coaching project, seek external perspectives or use outside coaches.

- Your built-in incentive to help the organization is a motivation to support your coaching clients—unless the results they are attempting to achieve are in conflict with the goals or priorities of functions, business units, or projects of which you are a part. Again, if this is the case, seek external perspectives or refer the client to another coach.

- It is natural to avoid approaches or solutions that have not worked in your organization in the past. But past failures may have less to do with the approach or solution and more to do with the circumstances and individuals involved. Be open to many possibilities while remaining realistic based on the current situation of your organization and its players. Also be vigilant: Don't allow any past biases or assumptions to prevent you from suggesting solutions that may work today. If you are convinced the approach is right, persist even when the option has not worked in the past and the organization is biased against it.

- As an internal human resources professional, you are an insider. This is a viewpoint that leads people to accept and trust you. But it can also serve as a barrier—the insider is rarely considered to be as expert as the outsider recognized in the field as such. Spotlight your experience with other organizations and best-in-class practices. Publish articles and books that give you that external credibility. Attend meetings and interact regularly with external experts; incorporate their advice into your coaching. To gain further credibility in your organization, reference and give ample credit to these other experts.

- You have a reputation in your organization. Most reputations have positive aspects on which to capitalize and more negative aspects to live down. You can't manage your reputation if you don't know what it is, so seek feedback from people you trust to tell you the truth about what they think and others say. Use an external 360-degree feedback process that maintains anonymity. Perception is not reality but may be seen as such, so balance it with hard data to give people the chance to change their perceptions about you. Until that happens, don't get hung up on negative feedback.

- If you have relied on associations with people or groups who are sources of power in your organization, those associations may backfire in executive coaching. When a coachee or others involved in a coaching project have doubts about your objectivity or neutrality, distance yourself from those associations or provide a reference to another coach.

- It is rare that internal human resources professionals can be effective coaching the most senior executives in their organizations. The executives may find it difficult to trust that what they tell you will remain completely confidential. And you yourself probably believe that, if you were to be completely honest and direct with the executive, it would hurt your career. Serving as the confidant and advisor to a senior leader usually changes the way others deal with you and makes it difficult for you to remain a regular member of the team. Before taking on senior leadership projects, consider your ability to best serve the executive. The coaching may change your feelings of satisfaction as part of the organization. You may also lose your role as a trusted colleague with whom people can be open.

TRANSITIONING FROM OTHER SPECIALTY FIELDS

If you determine that professional executive coaching is right for you, build a firm foundation of knowledge and skills. Then use your background and training in your specialty field to offer unique benefits and perspectives to your coaching clients.

Leaders and their organizations tend to be selective about their executive coaches, and that selectivity is often misguided. Many competent executive coaches are kept out of the running because they lack extensive experience. Others are chosen because they have a certification as an executive coach, often from a program that doesn't provide the in-depth education described earlier in this book. If you are certified as an executive coach but know little about business, psychology, organization development, or coaching principles or practices, get further education before hanging out your shingle. Don't pull the professional discipline down with shallow expertise.

Strategies for Transitioning from Other Specialty Fields

If you have the requisite knowledge and skill but cannot get hired because you lack significant experience as an executive coach, overcome this Catch-22 as follows:

- Don't limit how you think about and present yourself to others by the specialty field from which you have come. As long as you take off the blinders of that specialty and gain the needed competencies for professional executive coaching, you are an executive coach.
- Use what you know and what you have done. Slowly build your executive coaching experience by starting in industries, functions, or situations where you have the greatest experience. If you have coached politicians on making speeches, then begin your executive coaching work with political or government leaders. If you come from management in information

or high technology, then do executive coaching with would-be leaders in those areas. Slowly expand your coaching to leaders in other industries, functions, and situations.

- Don't be afraid to ask satisfied coaching clients to refer you to their colleagues.
- Don't be afraid to take on stretch assignments—but don't stretch so far beyond your growing capabilities that you put your client and your practice in jeopardy. It takes a very experienced executive coach to help a CEO, executive director, or board chairperson from a large organization revamp the way they do strategic planning and become more visionary and inspirational. Only highly experienced executive coaches should take on these types of coaching projects.
- If you have many years of experience in one specialty area, don't fool yourself into thinking that this irrelevant experience and wisdom will compensate for the knowledge and experience demanded by a special coaching situation.

Regardless of the specialty from which you are transitioning, executive coaching requires expertise in change management and resilience in the face of ambiguity, rejection, and a certain amount of failure as a newcomer. But if executive coaching is right for you, the end result will be truly satisfying. Use your natural strengths; your style, knowledge, skills, abilities, and experience. Don't try to go through the transition on your own—build and rely on a network of supporters, supervisors, and mentors. You don't need to be sure of your ultimate destination as you begin your journey. But with a general direction in mind, clarity of purpose, and commitment to the cause of building great leaders, you can make the transition a smooth one.

CHAPTER SIX

A Plan for Your Professional Executive Coaching Practice

Now that you have read this book in all or in part, and perhaps undertaken other activities to help you decide how to build and manage your professional executive coaching practice, use the plan in this chapter to document what you will do. Complete those sections of the plan that will be helpful to you. You can also use this plan to support your supervision of other executive coaches.

Today's snapshot of your practice may not have as much meaning to you now as it will in the months and years to come. Even if aspects of this plan seem obvious to you as you write them down, it is still worth documenting your thoughts for future reference as your plans evolve and change. It may also be helpful to share your plan with the people you rely on for professional networking or mentoring.

Given today's unsure, unpredictable world and business environment, it may be difficult to answer some of the questions in this plan. In such a case, develop the most likely scenario of what may happen and how you will build and manage your plan to work within each scenario. When you don't have enough data or confidence about what will happen or what you want to accomplish, develop some contingency plans to fall back on if you or your practice head in an unexpected direction.

Best of luck in developing and implementing your professional executive coaching plan!

Date: _____

Key Principles, Realizations, and Guidelines to Remember as You Build and Manage Your Executive Coaching Practice

Is Conducting a Professional Executive Coaching Practice the Right Choice for You?

The more positive answers you give to the following questions, the more executive coaching may be right for you. Besides considering your own self-perception as you answer these questions, be sure to get perspectives on you and your plan from people who know you well and whose opinions you value.

Your Needs

1. Is it important for you to change people's lives: both the leaders you coach and the people they lead and interact with?

   _____

2. Do you care about the success of organizations, their business results, and their return to key constituents?

   _____

3. Are your income needs aligned with executive coaching fees? Are you prepared to provide significant coaching

services for lower fees as a contribution to the mission or purpose of the organizations you will serve?

_____

Your Interests

1. Are you fascinated by leadership, organizational systems, and the intensity of the leader's role in organizations?

_____

2. Do you like to deal with high-pressure situations in which major organizational issues and key work relationships are dealt with openly and practically?

_____

3. Do you enjoy working one-on-one and in small groups with smart people? Do you have a deep desire to learn continually as you help others learn, change what they do, build their skills, and work more effectively?

_____

Your Abilities

1. Do you have mature self-confidence, humility, assertiveness, openness, and flexibility in what you do and how you do it?

_____

2. Do you have a reserve of positive energy, optimism, and resilience?

_____

3. Do you process information quickly, envision scenarios, understand how you and others think and feel, and build and manage relationships easily?

_____

Your Tendencies

1. Are you comfortable being independent while still collaborating with others to support shared goals?

_____

2. Are you geared to data and evidence to help people make decisions?

_____

3. Do you have an action orientation to solving problems, capitalizing on opportunities, and getting things done?

_____

Your Plan for Professional Development as an Executive Coach

Review your knowledge, skills, attributes, and abilities as recorded in the surveys in Chapter 2. Based on your self-assessment and any 360-degree feedback you have received, what are your strengths and opportunities for development as you prepare yourself for an executive coaching practice or continue to build your capabilities as an executive coach?

Greatest Strengths to Leverage

GREATEST STRENGTHS	WAYS TO LEVERAGE THESE STRENGTHS
Coaching knowledge	
Psychological knowledge	
Business acumen	
Organizational knowledge	
Executive coaching tasks and skills	
General attributes and abilities	

WHAT WILL YOU DO TO LEVERAGE YOUR STRENGTHS?

Check the strategies you will use in the coming year and describe how you will use them to leverage your strengths and build and manage your practice.

- ☐ Publish.
- ☐ Conduct research.
- ☐ Highlight your strengths in your promotional material.
- ☐ Do public speaking.
- ☐ Teach others.
- ☐ Consult or subcontract to other coaches.
- ☐ Develop a special consulting or coaching service.
- ☐ Develop tools and special materials to use in your practice.
- ☐ Post information and guides on your web site.
- ☐ Develop a Web-based or hard-copy newsletter.
- ☐ Form a professional association or group.
- ☐ Lead a conference.
- ☐ Sell targeted products or services.
- ☐ Select an area in which to become a recognized expert; use your existing strengths to build and market that expertise.

Great Opportunities for Professional Development as an Executive Coach

GREATEST OPPORTUNITIES FOR PROFESSIONAL DEVELOPMENT	WAYS TO DEVELOP IN THESE AREAS
Coaching knowledge	
Psychological knowledge	
Business acumen	

Organizational knowledge	
Executive coaching tasks and skills	
General attributes and abilities	

WHAT WILL YOU DO TO BUILD YOUR KNOWLEDGE OR SKILLS IN EXECUTIVE COACHING?

Check the strategies you will use in the coming year and describe how you will use them to develop professionally as an executive coach.

- ☐ Enroll in academic courses.
- ☐ Read.
- ☐ Take continuing education workshops.
- ☐ Work with a mentor.
- ☐ Hire your own coach.
- ☐ Work in collaboration with other coaches who are strong in the area in which you need development.
- ☐ Do research.
- ☐ Take on a stretch assignment.
- ☐ Work as an apprentice with an expert.
- ☐ Complete a certification or degree.
- ☐ Practice using a standard protocol.
- ☐ Observe yourself on videotape.
- ☐ Get feedback from clients.
- ☐ Get feedback from experts.
- ☐ Log or record journal entries to track your experiences and progress.
- ☐ Establish specific, time-driven, measurable development goals.
- ☐ Teach others.

- ☐ Attend conferences.
- ☐ Join a peer-supervision group.
- ☐ Hire a supervisor.
- ☐ Get a position in a consulting firm where you can be supervised and learn from other experts.
- ☐ Volunteer or provide reduced-fee services that give you the opportunity to build your skills.

Attributes or Gaps in Ability for Which to Compensate

Attributes or Gaps in Ability that Require Compensation	Ways to Compensate
Attributes	
Gaps in ability	

What Will You Do to Compensate for Your Attributes or Gaps in Abilities?

Check the strategies you will use in the coming year and describe how you will use them to compensate for your attributes or gaps in your abilities as an executive coach:

- ☐ Use structured systems.
- ☐ Build a toolbox to guide your coaching activities.
- ☐ Meet regularly with a coach, counselor, or supervisor to review your work and get objective feedback, guidance, and support.

- ☐ Develop new approaches that force you to do what does not come naturally to you (for example, active listening, assertiveness, relaxation, writing things down before responding, time management).
- ☐ Over-practice techniques until they become ingrained.
- ☐ Get coaching or counseling for "cognitive restructuring" to challenge your irrational or nonconstructive beliefs or assumptions.
- ☐ Learn new models of thinking to rely on when you are inclined to do something less constructive.
- ☐ Join a support group to share guidance, encouragement, and reinforcement for what you find difficult or uncomfortable but need to do.
- ☐ Choose coaching assignments that rely on your strengths rather than weaker areas where you are less able or have difficulty learning.
- ☐ Accept who you are and present yourself with what you do best instead of what you wish you did better.
- ☐ Rely on your secondary strengths.
- ☐ Be careful not to overuse or misuse your natural strengths.
- ☐ Reassess your old assumptions about yourself and your limitations as a reality check on what you can do.
- ☐ "Walk before you run" when you try new approaches or skills.
- ☐ Give yourself time to learn and change.
- ☐ Hire people to assist you in areas where you are less able or comfortable and don't want to learn or adapt (accounting, technology, marketing, writing, etc.).

Your Three-Year Professional Development Plan

DEVELOPMENTAL OPPORTUNITIES	WHAT TO DO THIS YEAR	WHAT TO DO NEXT YEAR	WHAT TO DO THE YEAR AFTER NEXT
Greatest strengths to leverage 1. 2. 3.			
Greatest opportunities for development 1. 2. 3.			
Greatest needs that require compensation 1. 2. 3.			

Personal, Career, and Business Goals and Requirements for Your Practice

YOUR PERSONAL GOALS

Answer the following questions to help you identify your personal goals for your professional executive coaching practice:

1. What do you value most in life: money, recognition, productivity, social contact, being in a certain environment, and so on?

   _____
   _____
   _____
   _____

2. What do you need to be comfortable and happy?

   _____
   _____
   _____
   _____

3. What nurtures and feeds you?

   _____
   _____
   _____
   _____

4. What do you want to give up or stop doing? Do you want to head in a different direction?

   _____
   _____
   _____
   _____

5. What contributions do you want to make to the world?

   _____
   _____
   _____
   _____

6. What do you wish you had accomplished in your life so far?

_____

_____

_____

_____

7. What have you done that has given you the greatest satisfaction?

_____

_____

_____

_____

8. Whom do you admire the most?

_____

_____

_____

_____

9. What are the gaps between the ideal you and who you are today?

_____

_____

_____

_____

10. What feedback regarding who you are as a person have you received from people you respect and care about?

_____

_____

_____

_____

11. What personal challenges do you face? Are there any conditions or limitations that you need to overcome or compensate for (physical, intellectual, stylistic, psychological, social)?

_____

_____

_____

_____
_____
_____

12. What personal assets do you want to leverage?

_____
_____
_____
_____

13. What do the people you want to please tell you to change about how you live your life and interact with them?

_____
_____
_____
_____

14. In the world at large, and in the smaller world in which you live, what bothers you most? Do you wish you could change it?

_____
_____
_____
_____

15. What causes do you want to support: social, political, spiritual, environmental, economic, and so on?

_____
_____
_____
_____
_____
_____

16. What unfulfilled personal goals have you had for many years?

_____
_____
_____
_____

17. How would you like to be seen by others?

_____
_____
_____
_____

18. What would make you proud?

_____
_____
_____
_____

19. What do others do that causes you to respect them?

_____
_____
_____
_____

20. What would you like to be remembered for?

_____
_____
_____
_____

YOUR CAREER GOALS

Answer the following questions to help you identify your career goals for your practice:

1. What interests you most? What fascinates or intrigues you?

_____
_____
_____
_____

2. What kinds of work activities do you most enjoy?

_____
_____
_____
_____

3. What are your greatest abilities, strengths, and talents that you would like to apply at work?

_____

_____

_____

_____

_____

4. For which work activities do you get the most positive feedback from others?

_____

_____

_____

5. What potential areas of competence would you like to develop?

_____

_____

_____

6. What types of people or their attributes do you deal with best?

_____

_____

_____

7. What do you imagine and dream about doing professionally?

_____

_____

_____

8. How do you measure your success at work? What measures are the most meaningful to you?

_____

_____

_____

_____

9. With which peers do you get the most satisfaction working?

_____

_____

_____

_____

10. What are your long-term career objectives? What do you want to accomplish? What do you want to become professionally?

_____

_____

_____

_____

11. How do you want to conduct yourself professionally as you strive to achieve your long-term career objectives (ethics, standards, relationships, etc.)?

_____

_____

_____

_____

_____

_____

12. What are your short-term career objectives? What do you want to accomplish, keep the same, or change in the next 2 to 3 years?

_____

_____

_____

_____

_____

_____

13. What work environments and cultures do you want to work in or avoid?

_____

_____
_____
_____

14. How independently do you want to work? Do you want to control what you do and how you do it, or follow the direction and standards of others?

_____
_____
_____
_____

YOUR BUSINESS GOALS AND REQUIREMENTS

Answer the following questions to help you identify your business goals and requirements for your practice:

1. What is your long-term vision for your coaching practice? What will it look like in 3 to 5 years?

_____
_____
_____
_____

2. What is the mission of your practice? What do you want to do? For whom? For what purpose?

_____
_____
_____
_____

3. What are your overall strategic goals 3 to 5 years out?

_____
_____
_____
_____

4. What approaches will you use to achieve those goals?

_____
_____

_____

_____

5. How will you apply those approaches?

_____

_____

_____

_____

6. What levels of leadership do you want to coach: board leaders, chief executives, middle managers, supervisors, professionals, others?

_____

_____

_____

_____

7. What industries do you want, and don't want, to work in?

_____

_____

_____

_____

8. What other products or consulting services will you provide apart from or together with your coaching services?

_____

_____

_____

_____

9. How will you generate leads?

_____

_____

_____

_____

10. How much profit do you want to clear on an annual basis—in the next year, 2 years, 3 years, and the longer term?

_____

_____

_____

_____

11. What other financial goals and requirements do you have for your practice? For example, do you want to build up assets to sell or pass on, minimize taxes, reduce overhead costs, reduce your reliance on other sources of income, generate revenue by managing other coaches?

_____

_____

_____

_____

12. How much are you able and willing to invest in building your practice in the next 1, 2, and 3 years? Consider infrastructure, materials, marketing and publicity, travel, professional support services (legal, accounting, insurance), time, and other resources.

_____

_____

_____

_____

13. What are your requirements and preferences about the form of your practice? Do you want to work as an employee coaching leaders and potential leaders in your organization? As an employee of a consulting or coaching firm? As an associate or adjunct coach who takes on coaching projects of that firm's clients? As an independent coach? As part of a formal or informal network or partnership of coaches?

_____

_____

_____

_____

14. If you want to work independently or in partnership with other coaches, in what form of legal entity do you want to practice? Options include sole proprietorship, partnership, professional corporation, C-corporation, S-corporation, limited liability company, and nonprofit entity. (See www.sba.gov for pros and cons of various business entities.)

_____
_____
_____
_____

15. What support staff will you employ to handle office management, administration, bookkeeping, tele-communications, technology, and so on?

_____
_____
_____
_____

16. Do you want to limit your practice? Will you only con-tract with organizations to coach their employees, or contract with individuals too? Will you restrict the indi-viduals or organizations for which you work (socially responsible organizations, geographic limitations, cer-tain types of coaching or coaching assignments, and the like)?

_____
_____
_____
_____

17. How will you limit or specialize your practice to work, or not work, with any organizational functions or depart-ments?

_____
_____
_____
_____

18. Do you want to limit the vehicles through which you will conduct coaching? Options include face-to-face, phone, videoconferencing, and e-mail or electronic dialogues.

_____
_____
_____
_____

19. If you do face-to-face coaching, will you limit where you will meet with your clients (at their offices, at your offices, off-site)?

_____
_____
_____
_____

20. How much of your time do you want to spend working (hours or days per week or month, months per year)?

_____
_____
_____
_____

21. How much work time will you commit to providing services at no or reduced cost, as a professional contribution or to give back to the community?

_____
_____
_____
_____

22. How will you charge your clients? By the project, time spent, results, retainer?

_____
_____
_____
_____

The Scope of Your Executive Coaching Practice

Check the services you plan to provide in your executive coaching practice:

- ☐ 360-degree interviews/surveys
- ☐ Assessments
- ☐ Feedback and development planning
- ☐ Team coaching
- ☐ High-potential coaching
- ☐ On-boarding coaching
- ☐ Remedial coaching
- ☐ Group coaching
- ☐ Legacy coaching
- ☐ Targeted coaching
- ☐ Coaching focused on interpersonal communication
- ☐ Coaching focused on strategic leadership
- ☐ Developmental coaching (focused on building self-awareness and removing internal individual barriers to success)
- ☐ Coaching focused on career development and career-life balance
- ☐ Coaching focused on building management skills and practices
- ☐ Coaching focused on achieving short-term, project-oriented results
- ☐ Specialized coaching in conjunction with organizational consulting
- ☐ Coaching internal and/or external coaches and human resources professionals on their coaching of others
- ☐ Other coaching services:

Your Professional Executive Coaching Value Proposition

Answer the following questions to define the value proposition for your practice:

1. What do you help leaders do?

_____
_____
_____
_____

2. How do you help them do it?

_____
_____
_____
_____

3. What knowledge, abilities, and skills make you especially capable of coaching leaders and would-be leaders?

_____
_____
_____
_____

4. What experience do you bring to help your clients?

_____
_____
_____
_____

5. What about you, who you are, how you think, your style, and how you work differentiates you as a professional executive coach?

_____
_____
_____
_____

6. What coaching services do you provide?

_____
_____

_____
_____

7. What types of people do you work best with? What about you and the way you work makes you the best coach for those clients?

_____
_____
_____
_____

8. What is your passion for coaching? Why do you coach, and what impact do you hope to achieve?

_____
_____
_____
_____

The Essential Building Blocks of Your Professional Executive Coaching Practice

YOUR COACHING REFERRAL AND CONSULTING NETWORK

Review the coaching services and areas of expertise, both in and out of coaching, from which to draw people for your referral and consulting network (see Chapter 4). Identify the people who will refer coaching projects to you, to whom you can refer coaching and consulting, and with whom you can consult. Make note of areas where you can find additional resources to fill any gaps in your network.

1. Professionals with areas of expertise stronger than yours:

_____
_____
_____
_____

2. Professionals who offer services you do not:

_____
_____
_____
_____

3. Professionals with different theoretical approaches than yours:

_____
_____
_____
_____

4. Professionals from different disciplines:

_____
_____
_____
_____

5. Professionals who offer the same services as you do, to whom you can make referrals when you are not available, need additional coaches to work with you or separately, or a conflict of interest or dual relationship exists:

_____
_____
_____
_____

6. Professionals who provide services other than executive coaching:

_____
_____
_____
_____

7. Other sources for referral or consulting:

_____
_____
_____
_____

A Plan for Your Professional Executive Coaching Practice

YOUR EXECUTIVE COACHING TOOLBOX

Review the tools in each of the following categories, discussed in Chapter 4. List the tools you already have and the ones you need to find, develop, or acquire.

General Executive Coaching Tools

1. Precoaching tools

   Tools you have:

   _____

   _____

   Types of tools you need to find, develop, or acquire:

   _____

   _____

2. Contracting tools

   Tools you have:

   _____

   _____

   Types of tools you need to find, develop, or acquire:

   _____

   _____

3. Assessment tools

   Tools you have:

   _____

   _____

   Types of tools you need to find, develop, or acquire:

   _____

   _____

4. Goal-setting tools

   Tools you have:

   _____

   _____

   Types of tools you need to find, develop, or acquire:

   _____

   _____

5. Tools for guiding and facilitating leadership development and the achievement of work

   Tools you have:

   _____

   _____

   Types of tools you need to find, develop, or acquire:

   _____

   _____

6. Tools to help transition from coaching to long-term development

   Tools you have:

   _____

   _____

   Types of tools you need to find, develop, or acquire:

   _____

   _____

7. Tools to achieve specific executive coaching goals

   Tools you have:

   _____

   _____

   Types of tools you need to find, develop, or acquire:

   _____

   _____

8. Career-life coaching tools

   Tools you have:

   _____

   _____

   Types of tools you need to find, develop, or acquire:

   _____

   _____

9. Communication coaching tools

   Tools you have:

   _____

   _____

Types of tools you need to find, develop, or acquire:

_____

_____

10. Developmental coaching tools
Tools you have:

_____

_____

Types of tools you need to find, develop, or acquire:

_____

_____

11. Leadership coaching tools
Tools you have:

_____

_____

Types of tools you need to find, develop, or acquire:

_____

_____

12. Management coaching tools
Tools you have:

_____

_____

Types of tools you need to find, develop, or acquire:

_____

_____

Your Office Infrastructure

Office Space

1. What office space do you need/want?

_____

_____

2. What office space do you already have to meet your needs and wants?

_____

_____

3. What additional or different office space do you need?

_____

_____

4. What will you do to get that additional or different office space?

_____

_____

_____

_____

Data and File Management

1. What data and file management systems, processes, equipment, software, professional help, and other resources do you need/want?

_____

_____

_____

_____

2. What data and file management infrastructure do you already have to meet your needs and wants?

_____

_____

_____

_____

3. What additional or different data and file management infrastructure do you need?

_____

_____

_____

_____

4. What will you do to get that additional or different data and file management infrastructure?

_____

_____

_____

_____

Financial Management (budgeting, Invoicing, Accounts Receivable, Accounting, etc.)

1. What financial management systems, processes, equipment, software, professional help, and other resources do you need/want?

_____
_____
_____
_____

2. What financial management infrastructure do you already have to meet your needs and wants?

_____
_____
_____
_____

3. What additional or different financial management infrastructure do you need?

_____
_____
_____
_____

4. What will you do to get that additional or different financial management infrastructure?

_____
_____
_____
_____

Technology and Your Virtual Office

1. What technology and virtual office infrastructure do you need/want?

_____
_____
_____
_____

2. What technology and virtual office infrastructure do you already have to meet your needs/wants?

_____

_____

_____

_____

3. What additional or different technology and virtual office infrastructure do you need?

_____

_____

_____

_____

4. What will you do to get that additional or different technology and virtual office infrastructure?

_____

_____

_____

_____

Access to Knowledge and Information outside Your Practice

1. What infrastructure do you need/want to be able to access knowledge and information outside your practice?

_____

_____

2. What infrastructure do already have to be able to access knowledge and information outside your practice?

_____

_____

3. What additional or different infrastructure do you need/want to be able to access knowledge and information outside your practice?

_____

_____

4. What will you do to get that additional or different infrastructure?

_____

_____

Managing Coaching Projects

1. What infrastructure do you need/want to manage coaching projects?

_____

_____

2. What infrastructure do you already have to manage coaching projects?

_____

_____

3. What additional or different infrastructure do you need to manage coaching projects?

_____

_____

4. What will you do to get that additional or different infrastructure to manage coaching projects?

_____

_____

PROFESSIONAL AND PEER SUPERVISION

Immediate Supervision (in Next 6 Months, or the First 6 Months of Your Practice)

1. What supervision do you need/want in the next 6 months?

_____

_____

_____

_____

2. What are the goals and measures of success of that supervision?

_____

_____

_____

_____

3. From/with whom do you want to get that supervision?

_____

_____

_____

4. How will you organize that supervision (how often, where, at what cost, with what agenda, etc.)?

_____

_____

Longer-Term Supervision (in the Following Year, or the Year after the First 6 Months of Your Practice)

1. What supervision will you need/want?

_____

_____

_____

2. What are the goals and measures of success of that supervision?

_____

_____

_____

3. From/with whom do you want to get that supervision?

_____

_____

_____

4. How will you organize that supervision (how often, where, at what cost, with what agenda, etc.)?

_____

_____

Coaching Research

How will you track and analyze what you do in your coaching, what impact it has, what you learn, and what others can learn from your experience and results?

_____

_____

_____

_____

Professional Coaching Publication

1. What information, experience, findings, resources, or ideas do you want to share with the professional coaching community in the next 1 to 2 years?

    _____

    _____

    _____

    _____

2. What media or publications will you use to communicate with the professional coaching community? How will you develop or gain access to those media or publications?

    _____

    _____

    _____

    _____

Management/Leadership Publication

1. What information, experience, findings, resources, or ideas do you want to share with managers, leaders, and would-be managers and leaders?

    _____

    _____

    _____

    _____

2. What media or publications will you use to communicate with the managers, leaders, and would-be managers and leaders? How will you develop or gain access to those media or publications?

_____
_____
_____
_____

Community Service

1. What passions, causes, or personal goals can you tap into in order to donate coaching services to leaders or potential leaders in your community (youth, environment, religious groups, political causes, cultural programs, etc.)?

   _____
   _____
   _____
   _____

2. Which of these service opportunities will you explore over the next year?

   _____
   _____
   _____
   _____

3. What criteria will you apply to select the opportunities for donating your services?

   _____
   _____
   _____
   _____

4. How much of your time will you dedicate to donating coaching services to your community?

   _____
   _____
   _____
   _____

5. How will you enlist other coaches to join you in your community service work?

_____

_____

_____

_____

A Plan to Transition into Executive Coaching from Your Other Specialties

Review the information in Chapter 5 on transitioning from other specialties.

1. What knowledge and skills will you leverage from your experience in your current or past specialties?

   _____

   _____

   _____

   _____

2. What biases or approaches from your previous specialties do you need to compensate for as you transition into executive coaching?

   _____

   _____

   _____

   _____

3. In what situations will you start to coach—what industries, functions, levels of management, geographic regions, and so on?

   _____

   _____

4. What strategy will you use to expand the scope of your practice from your initial coaching situations?

   _____

   _____

   _____

   _____

A Summary Plan for Your Professional Executive Coaching Practice

1. Short and long-term goals for your practice
   - Short-term (how long)

     _____

     _____

   - Long-term (how long)

     _____

     _____

2. What your practice will look like:
   - In 1 year

     _____

     _____

   - In 2 years

     _____

     _____

   - In 3 years

     _____

     _____

   - In 5 years

     _____

     _____

   - In 10 years

     _____

     _____

3. Measures of success for your practice:
   - Quantitative results

     _____

     _____

   - Qualitative measures of how you accomplish your goals

     _____

     _____

4. How you will monitor the progress of your practice:

_____

_____

_____

_____

5. Likely scenarios for what will happen in the development of your practice:

_____

_____

_____

_____

6. What you will do to increase the likelihood that your ideal scenario(s) will come to pass:

_____

_____

_____

_____

7. Your contingency plans (if things don't go as you hope and plan):

_____

_____

_____

_____

8. Your rewards for success:

_____

_____

_____

_____

9. Whom you will enlist as coaches and mentors for the implementation of your plan:

_____

_____

_____

_____

10. How you will enlist and involve your coaches and mentors over the course of your plan:

_____

_____

_____

_____

Practical Resources for Professional Executive Coaching

The following resources will help you build and manage your professional practice in executive coaching. I have compiled the list from my own experience as well as colleagues' recommendations throughout the world. These resources are accurate to the best of my knowledge as of the writing of this book. The listing is far from comprehensive: I have tried to select a representative set of resources that I and others have found especially useful. If an available resource is not listed, it is not a reflection of its lack of quality or value. Many of the resources are directly related to building and managing your practice; others you will find useful as you work with your clients.

BOOKS AND ARTICLES

Adams, M. (2004). *Change your questions, change your life*. San Francisco: Berret-Koehler.

Allen, D. (2001). *Getting things done: The art of stress-free productivity*. New York: Penguin.

Anderson, D., & Anderson, M. (2004). *Coaching that counts: Harnessing the power of leadership coaching to deliver strategic value.* Burlington, MA: Elsevier.

Argyris, C. (1993). *Knowledge for action.* San Francisco: Jossey-Bass.

Bacon, T., & Spear, K. (2003). *Adaptive coaching: The art and practice of a client-centered approach to performance improvement.* Mountain View, CA: Davies-Black.

Bennett, J. (2006). An agenda for coaching-related research: A challenge for researchers. *Consulting Psychology Journal, 58,* 240–248.

Bennett, J., & Craig, W. (2005). Coaching eye for the OD practitioner. *OD Practitioner, 37,* 29–34.

Bennett, J., & Martin, D. (2003). The next professional wave: Consultant/coach. *Consulting to Management, 12,* 6–8.

Bennis, W. (1997). *Why leaders can't lead.* San Francisco: Jossey-Bass.

Berger, P., & Luckmann, T. (1991). *The social construction of reality.* New York: Penguin.

Berglas, S. (2002). The very real dangers of executive coaching. *Harvard Business Review, 80,* 86–92.

Bergquist, W. H., Bergquist, W., Merritt, K., & Phillips, S. (1999). *Executive coaching: An appreciative approach.* Sacramento, CA: Pacific Soundings Press.

Bernstein, D., & Nash, P. (2006). *Essentials of psychology.* Boston: Houghton-Mifflin.

Betof, E., & Harwood, F. (1992). *Just promoted!* New York: McGraw-Hill.

Bianco-Mathis, V., Nabors, L., & Roman, C. (2002). *Leading from the inside out.* Thousand Oaks, CA: Sage.

Blattner, J., & Bacigalupo, A. (2007). Using emotional intelligence to develop executive leadership and team and organizational development. *Consulting Psychology Journal, 59,* 209–219.

Block, P. (1981). *Flawless consulting: A guide to getting your expertise used.* San Francisico: Jossey-Bass.

Appendix

Bohm, D., Nichol, L., & Senge, P. (2004). *On dialogue*. London: Routledge Classics.

Bork, D., Jaffe, D., Lane, S., Dashew, L., & Heisler, Q. (1996). *Working with family businesses: A guide for professionals*. San Francisco: Jossey-Bass.

Bossidy, L (2007). What your leader expects of you. *Harvard Business Review*, *85*, 58–65.

Bowles, S., & Picano, J. (2006). Dimensions of coaching related to productivity and quality of life. *Consulting Psychology Journal*, *58*, 232–239.

Boyatzis, R., Smith, M., & Blaize, N. (2006). Developing sustainable leaders through coaching and compassion. *Academy of Management Learning and Education*, *5*, 8–24.

Braun, M. (2005). *The presence process*. New York: Beaufort Books.

Brewer, J. (2005). *The psychology of executive coaching: The state of the art* [DVD]. San Francisco: Leadership Consulting Group. Available from jdavidbrewer@earthlink.net.

Bridges, W. (2003). *Managing transitions: Making the most of change*. Cambridge, MA: Perseus.

Buckingham, M., & Clifton, D. (2001). *Now, discover your strengths*. New York: The Free Press.

Butteriss, M., & Roiter, B. (2004). *Corporate MVPs: Managing your company's most valuable performers*. Toronto, Ontario, Canada: Wiley.

Buzan, T. (1993). *The mind map book*. New York: Penguin.

Carlson, R. (1998). *Don't sweat the small stuff workbook*. New York: Hyperion.

Carson, R. (2003). *Taming your gremlin: A surprisingly simple method for getting out of your own way*. New York: HarperCollins.

Cavanagh, A., Grant, A., & Kemp, T. (Eds.). (2005). *Evidence-based coaching: Contributions from the behavioral sciences* (Vol. 1) Bowen Hills, Queensland, Australia: Australian Academic Press.

Chait, R., Ryan, W., & Taylor, B. (2005). *Governance as leadership: Reframing the work of nonprofit boards*. Hoboken, NJ: Wiley.

Chapman, T., Best, B., & Van Casteren, P. (2003). *Executive coaching: Exploding the myths*. New York: Palgrave Macmillan.

Chernis, C., & Goleman, D. (Eds.). (2001). *The emotionally intelligent workplace: How to select for, measure, and improve emotional intelligence in individuals, groups, and organizations*. San Francisco: Jossey-Bass.

Chiodi, M. (2003). *The art of building people: 36 coaching tools for getting more out of work and life*. St. Paul, MN: Chiberry Press.

Ciampa, D., & Watkins, M. (1999). *Right from the start: Taking charge in a new leadership role*. Boston: Harvard Business School Press.

Cohen A., & Bradford, D. (2005). *Influence without authority*. Hoboken, NJ: Wiley.

Collins, J. (2001). *Good to great: Why some companies make the leap . . . and others don't*. New York: HarperCollins.

Collins, J., & Porras, J. (1997). *Built to last: Successful habits of visionary companies*. New York: HarperCollins.

Coutu, D. (2002). How resilience works. *Harvard Business Review, 80*, 46–50.

Covey, S. (1990). *The seven habits of highly effective people*. New York: Simon & Schuster.

Dotlich, D., & Cairo, P. (1999). *Action coaching: How to leverage individual performance for company success*. San Francisco: Jossey-Bass.

Douglas, C., & Morley, W. (2000). *Executive coaching: An annotated bibliography*. Greensboro, NC: Center for Creative Leadership.

Druckman, D., & Bjork, R. (1991). *In the mind's eye: Enhancing human performance*. Washington, DC: National Academy Press.

Dweck, C. (2000). *Self-theories: Their role in motivation, personality, and development*. Philadelphia: Psychology Press.

Ennis, S., Goodman, R., Hodgetts, W., Hunt, J., Mansfield, R., Otto, J., et al. (2005). *Core competencies of the executive coach*. Boston: Executive Coaching Forum.

Evers, W., Brouwers, A., & Welko, T. (2006). A quasi-experimental study on management coaching effectiveness. *Consulting Psychology Journal, 58*, 174–182.

Executive Coaching Forum. (2004). *The executive coaching handbook: Principles and guidelines for a successful coaching partnership* (3rd ed.) Boston: Author.

Fairley, S., & Stout, C. (2004). *Getting started in personal and executive coaching.* Hoboken, NJ: Wiley.

Fiarhurst, G., & Sarr, R. (1996). *The art of framing: Managing the language of leadership.* San Francisco: Jossey-Bass.

Fitzgerald, C., & Berger, J. (Eds.). (2002). *Executive coaching: Practices & perspectives.* Palo Alto, CA: Davies-Black.

Flaherty, J. (2005). *Coaching: Evoking excellence in others.* Oxford, England: Butterworth-Heinemann.

French, W., & Bell, C. (1978). *Organization development: Behavioral science interventions for organization improvement.* Englewood Cliffs, NJ: Prentice-Hall.

Galbraith, J., Downey, D., & Kates, A. (2002). *Designing dynamic organizations: A hands-on guide for leaders at all levels.* New York: AMACOM.

Gallwey, W. (1997). *The inner game of tennis: The classic guide to the mental side of peak performance.* Toronto, Ontario, Canada: Random House.

Garman, A., Whiston, D., & Zlatoper, K. (2000). Media perceptions of executive coaching and the formal preparation of coaches. *Consulting Psychology Journal, 52,* 203–205.

Gebelein, S., Lee, D., Nelson-Neuhaus, K., & Sloan, B. (1999). *Successful executive's handbook.* Minneapolis, MN: PreVisor.

Gebelein, S., Nelson-Neuhaus, K., Skube, C., Lee, D., & Stevens, L. (2006). *Successful manager's handbook.* Minneapolis, MN: PreVisor.

Gerard, G. (2001). *Dialogue at work.* Waltham, MA: Pagasus Communications.

Gladwell, M. (2005). *Blink: The power of thinking without thinking.* New York: Little, Brown.

Goldsmith, M., & Lyons, L. (2005). *Coaching for leadership: The practice of leadership coaching from the world's greatest coaches.* San Francisco: Wiley.

Goldsmith, M., & Reiter, M. (2007). *What got you here won't get you there*. New York: Hyperion.

Goleman, G. (1995). *Emotional intelligence*. New York: Bantam.

Goleman, G. (2000). *Emotional intelligence at work*. San Francisco: Jossey-Bass.

Green, J., & Grant, A. (2003). *Solution-focused coaching: Managing people in a complex world*. London: Momentum.

Hargrove, R. (2003). *Masterful coaching*. San Francisco: Jossey-Bass.

Harkavy, D. (2007). *Becoming a coaching leader*. Nashville, TN: Thomas Nelson.

Hart, E., & Kirkland, K. (2001). *Using your executive coach*. Greensboro, NC: Center for Creative Leadership.

Hart, V., Blattner, J., & Leipsic, S. (2001). Coaching versus therapy. *Consulting Psychology Journal, 53*, 229–237.

Heifetz, R., & Linsky, M. (2002). A survival guide for leaders. *Harvard Business Review, 80*, 65–74.

Hilburt-Davis, J., & Dyer, W. (2002). *Consulting to family businesses: Contracting, assessment, and implementation*. San Francisco: Jossey-Bass.

Hill, L. (2003). *Becoming a manager: Mastering the challenges of leadership*. Boston: Harvard Business School Press.

Hirsch, S. (2004). *Introduction to type and coaching*. Mountain View, CA: CPP, Inc.

Hudson, F. (1999). *The handbook of coaching*. San Francisco: Jossey-Bass.

Hunt, J., & Weintraub, J. (2002). *The coaching manager: Developing top talent in business*. Thousand Oaks, CA: Sage.

Hunt, J., & Weintraub, J. (2007). *The coaching organization: A strategy for developing leaders*. Thousand Oaks, CA: Sage.

Ibarra, H. (2004). *Working identity*. Boston: Harvard Business School Press.

Isaacs, W. (1999). *Dialogue: The art of thinking together*. New York: Doubleday.

Jeanneret, R., & Silzer, R. (1998). *Individual psychological assessment: Predicting behavior in organizational settings*. San Francisco: Jossey-Bass.

Jones, G., & Spooner, K. (2006). Coaching high achievers. *Consulting Psychology Journal, 58*, 40–50.

Katzenbach, J., & Smith, D. (2003). *The wisdom of teams*. New York: McKinsey.

Kegan, R., & Laskow, L. (2001). *How the way we talk can change the way we work*. San Francisco: Jossey-Bass.

Kilberg, R., & Diedrich, R. (Eds.). (2007). *The wisdom of coaching*. Washington, DC: American Psychological Association.
This book is a collection of some of the best articles on executive coaching printed in the *Consulting Psychology Journal: Practice and Research*. This reference is provided instead of listing all of the many significant articles reprinted in the book.

Kline, N. (1999). *Time to think*. London: Cassels Illustrated.

Kofodimos, J. (2007). *The executive coaching solution: Getting maximum benefit from your coaching experience*. Mountain View, CA: Davies-Black.

Kotter, J. (1996). *Leading change*. Boston: Harvard University Press.

Kouzes, J., & Posner, B. (1987). *The leadership challenge: How to get extraordinary things done in organizations*. San Francisco: Jossey-Bass.

Kouzes, J., & Posner, B. (1993). *Credibility: How leaders gain and lose it, why people demand it*. San Francisco: Jossey-Bass.

Kramers, K. (2002). *CEO tools: The nuts-n-bolts of business for every manager's success*. Stockbridge, GA: Gandy Dancer Press.

Law, H., Ireland, S., & Hussain, Z. (2007). *The psychology of coaching, mentoring and learning*. Chichester, West Sussex, England: Wiley.

Leeds, D. (1987). *Smart questions: The essential strategy for successful managers*. New York: Berkley.

Luce, D. (1996). *Time-out leadership: Daily reflections to maximize your leadership effectiveness*. Nashville, TN: Thomas Nelson.

Ludeman, K., & Erlandson, E. (2004). Coaching the alpha male. *Harvard Business Review, 82,* 58–67.

Maister, D. (2000). *True professionalism.* New York: Free Press.

Maister, D., Galford, R., & Green, C. (2002). *The trusted advisor.* New York: Free Press.

McCall, M. (1993). *High flyers: Developing the next generation of leaders.* Boston: Harvard Business School Press.

McClelland, D., & Burnham, D. (1995). Power is the great motivator. *Harvard Business Review, 81,* 117–126.

Mink, O., Owen, K., & Mink, B. (1993). *Developing high-performance people: The art of coaching.* Cambridge, MA: Perseus.

Morgan, H., Harkins, P., & Goldsmith, M. (Eds.). (2004). *The art and practice of leadership coaching: 50 top executive coaches reveal their secrets.* Hoboken, NJ: Wiley.

Nachmanovitch, S. (1990). *Free play.* New York: Penguin Putnam.

Nadler, D. (1997). *Champions of change: How CEO's and their companies are mastering the skills of radical change.* San Francisco: Jossey-Bass.

Nadler, D., Nadler, M., Lorsch, J., & Behan, B. (2005). *Building better boards: A blueprint for effective governance.* San Francisco: Jossey-Bass.

Olivero, G., Bane, K., & Kopelman, R. (1997). Executive coaching as a transfer of training tool. *Public Personnel Management, 26,* 461–469.

O'Neill, J. (1993). *The paradox of success: When winning at work means losing at life.* New York: Tarcher Putnam.

O'Neill, M. (2000). *Executive coaching with backbone and heart.* San Francisco: Jossey-Bass.

Orenstein, R. (2006). Measuring executive coaching efficacy? The answer was right here all the time. *Consulting Psychology Journal, 58,* 106–116.

Orenstein, R. (2007). *Multidimensional executive coaching.* New York: Springer.

Parks, S. (2005). *Leadership can be taught.* Boston: Harvard Business School Press.

Passmore, J. (2007). An integrative model for executive coaching. *Consulting Psychology Journal, 59,* 68–78.

Peltier, B. (2001). *The psychology of executive coaching: Theory and application.* Ann Arbor, MI: Sheridan.

Peterson, C. (2006). *A primer in positive psychology.* New York: Oxford Press.

Peterson, D. (2002). Management development: Coaching and mentoring programs. In K. Kraiger (Ed.), *Creating, implementing, and managing effective training and development* (pp. 160–191). San Francisco: Jossey-Bass.

Peterson, D., & Hicks, M. (1996). *Leader as coach: Strategies for coaching and developing others.* Minneapolis, MN: PreVisor.

Raelin, J. (2003). *Creating leaderful organizations: How to bring out leadership in everyone.* San Francisco: Berrett-Koehler.

Reichheld, F. (1996). *The loyalty effect.* Cambridge, MA: Harvard University Press.

Robinson, D., & Robinson, J. (1995). *Performance consulting: Moving beyond training.* San Francisco: Berrett-Koehler.

Rock, D. (2006). *Quiet leadership: Help people think better—Don't tell them what to do.* New York: HarperCollins.

Rogers, J. (2004). *Coaching skills.* Maidenhead, England: Open University Press.

Rogers, J. (2006). *Developing a coaching business.* Maidenhead, England: Open University Press.

Rosenberg, M. (2005). *Nonviolent communication: A language of life.* Encinitas, CA: Puddle Dancer.

Schiller, M., Holland, B., & Riley, D. (2001). *Appreciative leaders: In the eye of the beholder.* Chagrin Fall, OH: Taos Institute.

Schon, D. (1995). *The reflective practitioner: How professionals think in action.* New York: Basic Books.

Seagal, J. (1997). *Raising your emotional intelligence.* New York: Henry Holt.

Selligman, M. (1990). *Learned optimism.* New York: Knopf.

Senge, P. (2006). *The fifth discipline: The art and practice of the learning organization.* New York: Doubleday.

Senge, P., Kleiner, A., Roberts, C., Ross, R., & Smith, B. (1994). *The fifth discipline fieldbook*. New York: Doubleday.

Shein, E. (1969). *Process consultation: Its role in organization development*. Reading, MA: Addison-Wesley.

Sherman, S., & Freas, A. (2004). The wild west of executive coaching. *Harvard Business Review, 82*, 82–90.

Siebert, A. (2005). *The resiliency advantage*. San Francisco: Berrett-Koehler.

Silsbee, D. (2004). *The mindful coach: Seven roles for helping people grow*. Marshall, NC: Ivy River Press.

Skiffington, S., & Zeus, P. (2001). *The complete guide to coaching at work*. North Ryde, New South Wales, Australia: McGraw-Hill.

Skiffington, S., & Zeus, P. (2003). *Behavioral coaching: Building sustainable personal and organizational strengths*. Sydney, Australia: McGraw-Hill.

Somers, M. (2007). *Coaching at work: Powering your team with awareness, responsibility and trust*. San Francisco: Jossey-Bass.

Steele, F. (1982). *The role of the internal consultant*. Boston: CBI.

Stober, D., & Grant, A. (Eds.). (2006). *Evidence-based coaching handbook*. Hoboken, NJ: Wiley.

Stone, D., Patton, B., Heen, S., & Fisher, R. (1999). *Difficult conversations: How to discuss what matters most*. New York: Viking.

Tannen, D. (1990). *You just don't understand: Women and men in conversation*. New York: Ballentine.

Thomas, J., & Thomas, T. J. (2006). *The power of opposite strengths: Making relationships work*. Austin, TX: Thomas Concept.

Underhill, B., McAnally, K., Koriath, J., & Goldsmith, M. (2007). *Executive coaching for results*. San Francisco: Berrett-Koehler.

Valerio, A., & Lee, R. (2005). *Executive coaching: A guide for the HR professional*. San Francisco: Pfeiffer.

von Oech, R. (1998). *A whack on the side of the head: How you can be more creative*. New York: Warner.

Waldroop, J., & Butler, T. (2001). *The 12 bad habits that hold good people back*. New York: Random House.

Wasylyshyn, K., Gronsky, B., & Haas, J. (2006). Tigers, stripes, and behavior change: Survey results of a commissioned coaching program. *Consulting Psychology Journal, 58,* 65–81.

Watkins, M. (2003). *The first ninety days: Critical success strategies for leaders at all levels.* Boston: Harvard Business School Press.

West, L., & Milan, M. (2001). *The reflecting glass: Professional coaching for leadership development.* New York: Palgrave.

Wheatley, M. (2005). *Finding our way: Leadership for an uncertain future.* San Francisco: Berrett-Koehler.

Wheatley, M. (2006). *Leadership and the new science.* San Francisco: Berrett-Koehler.

Whitmore, J. (2002). *Coaching for performance* (3rd ed.) London: Nicholas Brealey.

Witherspoon, R., & White, R. (1997). *Four essential ways that coaching can help executives.* Greensboro, NC: Center for Creative Leadership.

Witworth, L., Kimsey-House, H., & Sandahl, P. (1998). *Co-active coaching: New skills for coaching people toward success in work and life.* Palo Alto, CA: Davies-Black.

Zenger, J., & Folkman, J. (2002). *The extraordinary leader: Turning good managers into great leaders.* New York: McGraw-Hill.

Zeus, P., & Skiffington, S. (2002). *The coaching at work toolkit: A complete guide to techniques and practices.* Sydney, Australia: McGraw-Hill.

JOURNALS

Coaching: An International Journal of Theory, Research, and Practice www.InformaWorld.com/coaching/

Consulting Psychology Journal: Practice and Research www.apa.org/journals/cpb/description.html

Harvard Business Review www.harvardbusinessreview.com

International Coaching Psychology Review www.psychology.org.au/units/interest_groups/coaching/

International Journal of Coaching in Organizations www.ijco.info/index/html

International Journal of Evidence Based Coaching and Mentoring www.brookes.ac.uk/schools/education/ijebcm/

International Journal of Mentoring and Coaching www.emccouncil.org/uk/journal.ntm/

ORGANIZATIONS

American Psychological Association www.apa.org

Association for Coaching www.associationforcoaching.com

Association for Executive Coaches and Supervisors www.apecs.org

Association for Professional Executive Coaching & Supervision www.apecs.org

Australian Psychological Society Interest Group in Coaching Psychology www.groups.psychology.org.au/igcp/

British Psychological Society Special Group in Coaching Psychology www.bps.org.uk/coachingpsy/coachingpsy_home.cfm

Center for Business as an Agent of World Benefit at Case Western Reserve http://worldbenefit.cwru.edu

Center for Creative Leadership www.ccl.org

Clinton Global Initiative www.clintonglobalinitiative.org

Coaches and Mentors of South Africa www.comensa.org.za/

Coaching and Mentoring Network www.coachingnetwork.org.uk/

Consortium for Research on Emotional Intelligence in Organizations (Rutgers) www.eiconsortium.org

Council on Executive Coaching The Conference Board www.conference-board.org/councils/councilsDetailUS.cfm?Council_ID=155&CFID=10613736&CFTOKEN=c29ade161764e739-AF873C26-B3FC-659C-8E5AF1F6FA700285/

European Mentoring and Coaching Council www.emcouncil.org

Foundation of Coaching www.thefoundationofcoaching.org

Global Coaching Convention www.coachingconvention.org

Graduate School Alliance for Executive Coaching www.gsaec
.org

Institute of Leadership and Management www.i-l-m.com

International Association of Coaches www.certifiedcoach.org

International Coaching Federation www.coachingfederation
.com

International Consortium for Coaching in Organizations www
.coachingconsortium.org

New England Society for Applied Psychology www.nesap.org

OD Network www.odnetwork.org

Skoll World Forum on Social Entrepreneurship www.skoll
.org

Society of Consulting Psychology www.div13.org

Society for Human Resource Management www.shrm.org

Society of Industrial and Organizational Psychology www.siop
.org

Society of Industrial and Organizational Psychology of South
Africa www.siopsa.org.za/

Work Life Research Centre www.workliferesearch.org/wl_site/
hp_main.htm

World Association of Business Coaches www.wabccoaches.com

OTHER WEB SITES

www.boardforum.org/boardcafe/

www.bps.org.uk/sub-sites$coachingpsy/articles/articles_home
.cfm

www.coachingandmentoringnetwork.co.uk/

www.coachville.com

www.ecoach.com

www.executivecoachingforum.com

www.managementhelp.org

www.peer.ca/

www.thesystemsthinker.com

www.viastrengths.org

Assessments, Tools, and Other Resources

Aspen Institute Programs http://fora.tv/partner/Aspen_Institute/ International nonprofit organization dedicated to fostering enlightened leadership and open-minded dialogue

Bar-On EQi www.mhs.com Emotional competency assessment

The Behavioral Wellness Program www.stressdirections.com

Benchmarks www.ccl.org/leadership/assessments/360-degree survey

"Creating Social Networks" (Mp3 recording) www.coachingto wardhappiness.com/CatherineFitzgerald.mp3/

DISC www.inscapepublishing.com or www.ttifdisc.com Assessment

FIRO-B (assessment) www.cpp.com/products/firo-b/

Gallup Strengths Finder Instrument *Now Discover Your Strengths* (pp. 76–82) New York: Free Press, 2000

The Leadership Architect Sort Cards (and associated materials) www.leadershiparchitect.com

Leadership Practices Inventory www.leadershipchallenge.com 360-degree survey

LSI 1 www.humansynergistics.com Assessment

MBTI www.cpp.com/products/mbti/Assessment

MSCEIT www.eiskills.com Emotional intelligence assessment

The Profiler for Leaders www.personneldecisions.com.sg/offer ings/profilor_leaders.asp 360-degree survey

16 PF www.ipat.com Personality assessment

Strong Interest Inventory www.cpp.com/products/strong/ Assessment

Tools for executive coaching www.executivecoachingforum .com Executives' tools, tools for the executive's organizations, resources, and research

Values in Action (VIA) Inventory of Strengths www.value sinaction.org

Voices Report www.ccl.com 360-degree survey

References

Betof, E., & Harwood, F. (1992). *Just promoted!* New York: McGraw-Hill.

Burns, J. M. (1978). *Leadership*. New York: Harper.

Chernis, C., & Goleman, D. (Eds.). (2001). *The emotionally intelligent workplace: How to select for, measure, and improve emotional intelligence in individuals, groups, and organizations*. San Francisco: Jossey-Bass.

Ennis, S., Goodman, R., Hodgetts, W., Hunt, J., Mansfield, R., Otto, J., et al. (2005). *Core competencies of the executive coach*. Boston: Executive Coaching Forum. Available from www.executivecoachingforum.com.

Executive Coaching Forum. (2004). *The executive coaching handbook: Principles and guidelines for a successful coaching partnership* (3rd ed.) Boston: Author.

Fitzgerald, C., & Berger, J. G. (Eds.). (2002). *Executive coaching practices and perspectives*. Palo Alto, CA: Davies-Black.

Graduate School Alliance for Executive Coaching. (June 11, 2007). *Guidelines for graduate academic programs in executive coaching*. Columbus, OH: GSAEC. Available from www.gsaec.org/curriculum.html.

Hunt, J., & Weintraub, J. (2002). *The coaching manager: Developing top talent in business*. Thousand Oaks, CA: Sage.

Seligman, M. E. P. (2002). *Authentic happiness: Using the new positive psychology to realize your potential for lasting fulfillment*. New York: Free Press.

Valerio, A. M., & Lee, R. J. (2005). *Executive coaching: A guide for the HR professional*. San Francisco: Wiley.

Index

225

Index

Index